• HAZELDEN MEDITATIONS •

Easy Does It

A Book of Daily 12 Step Meditations

Hazelden Publishing
Center City, Minnesota 55012
hazelden.org/bookstore

First published by Glen Abbey Books, Inc. 1990
First published by Hazelden Foundation 1999
Printed in the United States of America

ISBN: 978-1-56838-507-5

Editor's note

In the process of being reissued in 2019, *Easy Does It* has undergone minor editing updates and been retypeset in the Whitman font family.

INTERIOR DESIGN: TERRI KINNE
TYPESETTING: PERCOLATOR GRAPHIC DESIGN

This book is dedicated
to
NEWCOMERS

Introduction

"Easy does it" is a slogan and a philosophy of all Twelve Step fellowships. Those who work toward progress in recovery are advised to be patient. When they go slowly—and solutions to problems and situations begin to appear—they can take action.

"Easy does it" reminds one not to rush the program faster than it can go, but to grow *into* the program. Waiting patiently and carefully is not procrastinating. Every moment spent learning is an investment in the knowledge that one is finding the right answers.

"Easy does it" is not about being lazy. It is about working on slowing down and taking life on life's terms. It is simply being tuned into the secret of how recovery and life actually work.

This book is for members of all Twelve Step fellowships dedicated to a sane and manageable way of life, free of addictions, compulsions, and dependencies.

The "Keep it simple" manner in which this book is written will help newcomers with the basics of the program. Members who have more time in recovery will also benefit. As old-timers often say, "We never stop learning. As we will always be a student in our program, we remain teachable, we continue to open our minds to accept and our hearts to understand."

The program suggests to Twelve Step members that they have a quiet time each morning and "dress their minds as carefully as they dress their bodies." These daily recovery readings will guide you in planning and organizing positive thoughts and attitudes as each day begins.

At the end of the book is an inventory checklist and an index, which allows you to use this book at any time to check a topic and gather helpful insight. *The Twelve Step Prayer Book,* a companion book to *Easy Does It,* provides a collection of the best-loved prayers used by Twelve Step members for your prayer life.

May these daily readings help you in the morning, throughout your day, and on your journey with your fellow travelers.

—*Bill Pittman*

Serenity Prayer

God grant me the serenity
To accept the things I cannot change;
The courage to change the things I can;
And the wisdom to know the difference.

Living one day at a time;
Enjoying one moment at a time;
Accepting hardship as the pathway to peace;

Taking, as He did,
this sinful world as it is,
not as I would have it;
Trusting that He will
make all things right
if I surrender to His Will;

That I may be
reasonably happy in this life,
and supremely happy with Him
forever in the next.

Amen.

JANUARY

A New Beginning

The new is but the old come true; each sunrise sees a New Year born.

—Helen Hunt Jackson

We know that a totally new life can begin on any day of a year, at any hour of the day, or at any moment of an hour. Our new life began the moment we decided to surrender and admit to a powerlessness over a substance or an impulse. It began when we accepted the fact that we needed help and could receive it simply by asking.

Many of us used to choose New Year's Day as a time for making good resolutions and swearing off bad habits. When we failed, we simply shrugged and said, "Maybe I can start tomorrow, next week—or next New Year's Day." We were always going to "turn over a new leaf."

Now, in recovery, we no longer depend on doing it all alone. We know we can stay abstinent only by sharing with fellow members.

Let me remember, each day in recovery is another milestone. I no longer have to use a calendar.

• JANUARY 2 •

Jealousy

Beware of jealousy. It is the green-eyed monster which doth mock the meat it feeds on.

— William Shakespeare

As we aim toward a lasting and comfortable recovery, we may find that jealousy and envy get in our way. Sometimes they are combined with other enemies of good living like pride, self-will, dishonesty, hatred, selfishness, and resentment.

Jealousy is a danger in recovery. The kind of thinking that causes jealousy makes us believe that the world owes us much more than we are able to earn by our own best efforts.

When we envy others for what they own, for their standing in the community, or for the people who care about them, we are on our way to self-pity. This state of mind produces not only jealousy, depression, and an attitude that "life's not fair," but also anger against the world. Soon that jealousy and anger turn against those people most dear to us.

I am reminded that the Big Book calls jealousy "that most terrible of human emotions."

• JANUARY 3 •

Give with Humility

The greatest pleasure I know is to do a good act in secret and have it found out by accident.

—*Anonymous*

There is one bit of advice that is given in many ways to those of us in recovery. That advice is that we should give to others without looking for any credit for our generosity. To give something for the sheer joy of giving is the strongest step we can take in achieving the humility that is so vital to us. Humility is essential to our spiritual progress, and our spiritual progress is a necessary part of our recovery.

The encouragement to serve without seeking praise comes to us in many forms and from many places. Ancient wisdom advises us not to let our right hand know what our left hand is doing, and not to "sound a trumpet" to announce a good deed.

Let me learn to give without seeking credit. This is a humble act. It will result in the uplifting reward of humility, which is vital to my spiritual growth.

Helping Others

Gratitude should go forward,
rather than backward.

—Bill W.

When we realize how much the program and others have helped us, it becomes our responsibility to help others. Our Twelfth Step suggests we carry the message to those who still suffer. Many of our fellows are also suffering in recovery. We need to remember to help those who may need our fellowship as well as those in our fellowship.

Life is no longer a dead end without hope. With the gifts we have received from the program, we are able to help others. Our spiritual progress is easily measured by our positive actions. We are only asked to be helpful and leave the results to our Higher Power.

Bill W. said, "If you carry the message to still others, you will be making the best possible repayment for the help given you." I want to give back what I have received by sharing the program with others.

Musts

Not what we would, but what we
must makes up the sum of living.
—Richard Henry Stoddard

"We must do the things we must" is frequent advice in the program. Each Step is evidence of what our founders did in order to achieve abstinence and keep it going with serenity and security. All of the "musts" implied in the Steps and frequently mentioned throughout the Big Book are also spiritual. We will find the importance of "must" in the favorite quotes from that book.

The Steps aren't based on the theory of "thou shalt not." They are based on the theory that "thou shall." That's why we say "there are no musts" in our program.

Fortunately, those Twelve Steps we work require positive action. They tell us what we can do in order that each of us can live a joyous, happy, and free existence.

"Must" appears many times in the Big Book,
along with a few "absolutes." This doesn't refer
to my requirements for working the program.
It just lets me concentrate on what I can do,
not on what I can't.

Kindness

Little deeds of kindness, little words of love, help to make earth happy.
—Julia A.F. Carney

No act of kindness is ever too small to serve a good purpose. Oceans are made possible by little drops of water. Beaches are formed by tiny grains of sand. Slowly but surely, small efforts combine to help, encourage, and lead others to an ocean of success.

Small acts make large contributions to our spiritual growth. Newcomers to our program are advised that they can rid themselves of hatred, envy, resentments, and dislikes by using little acts and words to create a great turnaround in behavior. For instance, we are told, "Start forgiveness by praying for those you think have harmed you." This small act of prayer removes powerful negative emotions and replaces them with the wonder of serenity.

I shall try to be a little kinder and a little blinder to the faults of those around me.

Wanting God

God becomes directly and actively concerned with us humans when we want Him enough.
—Norman Vincent Peale

In writing about the Twelve Steps in the magazine *Guideposts*, Norman Vincent Peale stated, "Quite suddenly I saw that the power in (those steps) could be tapped by anyone wrestling with a power stronger than self. The Twelve Steps are a channel through which we can direct our appeal to the one Power that can lift the burden from us no matter what that burden is."

The Twelve Steps can be successfully applied to solving problems caused by any obsession or dependency. Regardless of age, background, or any other difference among members, the Steps lead to admitting and accepting a need, finding a Higher Power, turning problems over to God as we understand Him, pinpointing defects of character, making amends, reducing our defects, and learning to find God's will for us by prayer and meditation.

I am learning to let God further into my life.

Smile Again

'Tis easy enough to be pleasant
When life flows along like a song.
But the man worth while
Is the man who can smile
When everything goes dead wrong.
—*Emily Wheeler Wilcox*

We can truthfully, gratefully, and humbly say, "because of my recovery program, I can smile again." An addictive substance wipes smiles from the faces of men and women who become addicted. With honesty and thankfulness, we can say that the worst problems we face in recovery would have been a lot worse if we were still using.

In our new lives, even when everything goes dead wrong, we have learned to weigh any disaster against what it would have been like if we were still using. We are always aware that, if we smile while sharing with another, the hurt can become a lesson, and they, too, can smile again.

Recovery assures me that, while into each life some rain must fall (and sometimes, it's a torrent), behind the clouds the sun is still shining brightly. Bright days always come.

Futility of Hatred

Hating people is like burning down
your own home to get rid of a rat.
—Henry E. Fosdick

Hatred has many ancestors, and it breeds many vicious offspring. It's easy to hate someone, some thing, or some idea. That hatred gives birth to anger, resentment, envy, impatience, and fear. It soon becomes obvious to the newcomer that, by holding on to hatred, they are also breeding these other negative emotions as well.

Like a compulsion or addiction of any kind, hatred always gets worse unless we stop feeding it. When we indulge in hatred, we are unable to justify the savage feelings we experience. So we add anger, fear, and all the rest in order to fill the gap, but it's never enough. The result is always a need for more hatred, which crowds all the positive areas of our lives with negative emotions.

The time I spend on hatred can be
better used in working my program.

First Things First

Heaven is not reached by a single bound.
But we build the ladder by which we rise.
—J.G. Holland

The old saying "Rome was not built in a day" tells us that every great achievement must have a single beginning and must continue to be built with care. So it is understandable that in recovery we need to be reminded that all good endings depend on a careful, useful, and productive program of progress.

Our recovery brings us the best things in life, but we must never be greedy with them. Our appetite for the good things is great, but it should never become so great that we stop tasting each step of progress like we would taste each bite of a good dinner.

It is exciting to lose the desire for our addictive substance, but we must always stay alert to overconfidence. Carelessness can tell us, "You've got it made; you're free."

Today I'll remember that many a relapse has been a complete and painful surprise. "First things first" and "Easy does it" must always be my guides.

• JANUARY 11 •

Seeking Wisdom

He who knows and knows he knows,
he is wise—Follow him!

—Arabian saying

In the beginning of practicing the principles of our program, a complete understanding of them and knowing why they work is not really important. Sponsors usually tell a newcomer, "Just do it!" and "Fake it 'til you make it!" Analyzing "why" may become important later. But in the beginning, we accept advice blindly because the friends who teach us are, themselves, examples of why the principles work.

The program we follow is a simple one. All we need to do is know that the Steps work, and follow that knowledge. Those who find comfortable recovery know that what they've learned has been basically simple facts about themselves and their obsessive illness.

Learning the simple facts of my illness and
practicing the principles of my program
will lead to wisdom and lasting recovery.

Optimism

The optimist proclaims that we live in the best of all possible worlds, and the pessimist fears that this is true.

—James Branch Cabell

Optimists say that there are far more successes than failures in recovery. Pessimists say the opposite. The program says that anyone in recovery is a success. The program never fails, but individuals do because they give up too easily and too quickly.

When we decide to work closely with others, we have already declared that we will be optimistic about succeeding. During our excessive years, we suffered all the pessimism we ever again want to suffer. When we gather at a meeting, we are former pessimists who join in being optimists about winning. The irony is that this makes us winners.

Two people were served hamburgers for lunch. The pessimist muttered, "What a small dab of meat," while the optimist exclaimed, "What a big bun they serve here."

Be Positive

Two men look out through bars. One sees the mud, the other the stars.

—Frederick Langbridge

When we tell ourselves we can't progress, we are making sure we never can. We need to remember that success breeds success. A feeling of "I can do it" meant success in the important action of finding a Higher Power. After that, we could turn over our problems to that Higher Power. That accomplished, we could recognize our shortcomings and the release of their possession of us. Then we could make amends to those we had harmed. We continued to pray and meditate, and finally could give of what we had in serenity and security to others who suffered our problems.

Recovery places the accent on the positive side of involvement and effort. A negative approach creates a feeling of being a loser, which causes extra problems in itself.

Today I will say only positive things, or I will say nothing at all.

Service

Love is the forgetting of oneself
in the service of another.
—R. Ainsley Barnwell

Any act of "carrying the message" can serve a useful purpose, whether or not we see the results. Our home group carries the message and observes the Fifth Tradition.

If we maintain an attitude of being of service with love, we can work wonders at any time and every moment of a day. Through our Twelve Step program, we become aware that we have the opportunity of being an example of happy, joyous, and free living without the crutch of our addiction. This "face" we present can be a positive model for anyone who comes in contact with us.

If we confine our activities to only those persons who seek our help, we might miss the chance of influencing someone who isn't the direct target of our "service of love."

Today I will use the gifts my Higher Power
and the program have given me to be
of service to others.

Playing God

He was like the cock who thought the sun had risen to hear him crow.

— George Eliot

Ego and conceit are familiar words to all of us. Self-centered and ego-inflated obsessions created the idea within our confused minds that we could control everyone and everything. We in recovery refer to that as "trying to play God."

The world's great men and women credit their successes to the realization that they could not rule all of humankind. Those who never learned went down in disaster, as history proves.

The lives of the great remind us that we can make our lives inspiring and leave footprints in the sands of time. We only need to follow their example of choosing to be trusted servants rather than arrogant tyrants.

Our program teaches us that spiritual growth comes mainly from working in a simple manner with others as a team, all with a single purpose.

One of the elementary reasons why I am told to work at my conscious contact with my Higher Power is so that I can stop the mistake of trying to play God.

Change

You don't get to choose how you're going to die. Or when. You can only decide how you're going to live. Now.

—*Joan Baez*

Our life in recovery brings us a new attitude toward change. We remember the heartbreaking battles we fought as we resisted each new opportunity to change. We held on to old habit patterns even if they produced great pain in our lives. Somehow we found what we thought was a safe place in our addiction and our hopeless condition.

Our recovery has opened our eyes to a new world. We know deep in our hearts that our Higher Power wants only good things for us. We understand that change is to be welcomed like each new season. Our program teaches us that the unknown is not to be cursed, that God is revealed to us at such times. We come to trust our recovery.

I know that times of trouble will be followed by times of calm. I now welcome the changes that come into my life as new opportunities.

Honesty

Honesty's the best policy.
—Miguel de Cervantes

How grateful we became when we moved out from the shadows of our past. Our program asked us to be honest. We found that truth shone a bright light on our road to recovery. We could see all the little ways we had shaded the truth to serve our own ends. We could also see the awful pain this truth-twisting had caused us. We discovered there really was no such thing as a half-truth. There is either the truth or a lie.

Honesty is the bedrock of a life of recovery. Without honesty we lose our contact with our Higher Power. Without our Higher Power we lose our shield from our addiction. Without our shield we are hopelessly vulnerable to relapse. We are asked to be honest in all our affairs. This means we are careful to think before we speak and to guard against exaggeration.

At the conclusion of each day, I review my actions and ask myself if I have been honest in all I have said and done. Honesty in recovery takes practice, so I practice as if my life depended on it. It does.

Miracles

Chance is perhaps the pseudonym of God when he did not wish to sign.

—Anatole France

Chance is that unplanned and unexpected happening that brings happiness and freedom to us. It is often another name for a miracle.

Miraculous good fortune comes to all of us when we work our program. We accept the miracles of chance (luck) with gratitude. In fact, we help to make our own miracles by constant attention to thinking and behaving to the best of our ability and within our limitations, and by staying open to our Higher Power's will for us.

We make positive efforts to deserve the fortunes of chance. We cannot depend on luck, but must try to become receptive to the good things that happen to us. We accept the fact that, in recovery, miracles happen not to just a few at rare times, but to all of us, often.

I am learning in my program that I must never depend on miracles to solve my problems. But I can create the emotional and spiritual climate within myself for them to occur by working my program.

Self-Examination

And the night shall be filled with music
And the cares that infest the day
Shall fold their tents like the Arabs
And as silently steal away.
—Henry Wadsworth Longfellow

Our nights once were the horror hours. Too often, our "friendly substance" had been exhausted, and we could only sob in anguish and cry out, "God help me."

In recovery, many of us use those relaxing periods after going to bed for an examination of our victories and errors during the day that has just passed. These are the moments for seeking, through prayer and meditation, a more conscious contact with our Higher Power.

We examine what God's will is for us and plan to carry it out. We devote time to meditating on the gifts recovery has brought us. We learn more about how to work and to profit from the Steps.

Solitude is a time to know my acts and thoughts.
Have I sought gratitude and humility?
Have I been helpful to others without seeking recognition? Have I been honest?

Lovely Thoughts

What is lovely never dies, but passes into other loveliness.

—Thomas Bailey Aldrich

Thinking lovely thoughts during recovery encourages lovely acts. It is true that what starts as lovely will produce an air of loveliness around those of us who work for spiritual things. Truth has a relationship with lovely deeds. John Keats wrote that "beauty is truth and truth beauty," and also gave us the familiar words, "A thing of beauty is a joy forever."

Our thoughts determine the way we behave and shape the personal image that we pass on to those around us. There is an "outer show of an inner glow" that results from kindness and beauty of mind. Unhealthy thoughts or false fronts are destructive. We are what we think we can be and want to be. If we recognize the best and most healthy in the world around us, we will be worthy of the honest image others have of us.

Let me think only the best thoughts so that I might be the best I can be.

Higher Power

Our need is God's opportunity!
—Anonymous

Finding a Higher Power is as simple as seeking God. We learn in our Twelve Step program that God can, and will, lead us to solutions if He is sought. Such a search need be only fifteen inches—the distance from brain to heart.

We must feel, as well as recognize, our Higher Power. We will never fully understand God. If God were within human understanding, God would never be great enough to grant us our needs. Our first gift from a Higher Power was the capacity to know and accept the truth that we were not running our entire world.

It took us many years of running the show before we realized that all our human effort could not help us with our addiction.

I not only thank God for my program, but I thank the program for bringing me to God.

Healthy Pride

Pride works from within; it is the direct appreciation of oneself.

—Arthur Schopenhauer

Pride should not be feared. It is listed among the "seven deadly sins," but that is arrogance or false pride, not healthy pride that is a necessary part of self-esteem. Our program teaches us that the pride that "goes before a fall" is an unhealthy state, a symptom of egotism, grandiosity, and arrogance.

No harm will come to spiritual growth from the pride experienced when we freely admit to ourselves that any accomplishment of ours was not made by us alone. Humble pride acknowledges the guidance of others and faith in a Higher Power whom we call upon for inspiration and motivation.

With humility and God's help, I can learn to have healthy pride in my accomplishments and growth in the program.

Regrets

Opportunities flit by while we sit regretting the chances we have lost, and the happiness that comes to us we heed not, because of the happiness that is gone.

—*Jerome K. Jerome*

All of us have things we regret. But when regret takes possession of our thoughts and lives, we are in trouble. There's nothing wrong with playing the "what if" game, as long as it remains a game.

"What if I had chosen a different career? What if I hadn't (or had) married? What if I had traveled more? Where and who would I be today?" These are questions we all ask ourselves.

But the answer to unhappiness today doesn't lie in past decisions. If we think it does, we're ignoring the fact that each day is a new beginning. To concentrate on lost opportunities or to wish the past was different opens the door to despair. All we can do is the best we can do at any given moment.

Perhaps my life would have been different had I made different choices, but can I really say it would have been better? Who I am today is the person with whom I have to deal.

• JANUARY 28 •

Forgiveness

Forgiveness is another word for letting go.

—Matthew Fox

What a wonderful discovery it is when we realize our Higher Power has forgiven our past actions! What a joy to know that as we have been delivered from our addiction, we also have been forgiven for our mistakes! We experience a love we never dreamed possible, one that accepts us for being exactly who we are and doesn't put us down for all the trouble and pain we have caused.

As we have been forgiven, so must we forgive. Our program instructs us as to how we can receive our forgiveness and how we can extend forgiveness to others. Forgiveness is to recovery as oxygen is to the air we breathe.

We seek to get rid of all the conditions we place on our ability to forgive. There are no "ifs" in forgiveness. "If he apologizes first" or "if she changes her ways" are some of the ways we put conditions on forgiveness.

I realize that to keep my own forgiveness,
I must give it away. Forgiveness is for sharing.

The Blues

How do you know when you've hit bottom?
When you stop digging!

—*Anonymous*

We learn in recovery how to deal with the down times. Our program constantly reminds us that we hit bottom when we stop digging. Therefore, we can stop a downward spiral by simply letting go and letting God and our friends help us. Our Higher Power and the program will provide a ladder with which we can crawl out of our hole. We just need to remember to use the ladder.

God will never take away our free will. If we use our will to do the business of our Higher Power and work the Steps, we will be surrounded by love and have strength. It is when we sometimes use our free will to do the bidding of our own ego and set expectations too high that we fall into a bottomless pit.

Working with and helping others is the basic "ladder" at my disposal when I deal with the blues and down times. So I always keep in touch with my fellow travelers.

Faith

The reason why birds can fly and we can't is simply that they have perfect faith, for to have faith is to have wings.

—James M. Barrie

Blind faith in a Twelve Step program was all many of us had to our credit when we began recovery. Today we know it is our most valuable asset in the search for spiritual progress. Faith gives us an open mind, something we will always need. With the acceptance of our program's living principles comes the gift of belief.

The proof that our program works comes plentifully through all that we hear and read. We see God working through us and through others in our program. This is all the evidence we need for faith that God exists. Without an early child-like faith, the road toward peace of mind can be discouragingly rough.

I must believe that good things can happen and have faith that they will. Let me not forget that the absence of faith is despair.

Happiness

If it is happiness you want, change yourself, not other people. It is easier to protect your feet with shoes than to carpet the whole earth.

—Anonymous

"Happiness" is one of the three spiritual characteristics that the program tells us God wants for us. The other two are "joyous" and "free." In our study of what comes to us during our recovery, we read often about the treasured state of being happy. Someone wrote that we "have no more right to consume happiness without producing it than to consume wealth without producing it."

We in the program are not selfish with the happiness we gain through our own efforts and through the sharing of our fellow members. We hope that all around us can be as happy as our program has made us. A happy state of mind is contagious. Happiness breeds satisfaction—with ourselves, our fellow travelers, and life as a whole. It is difficult to be successful without finding happiness.

I accept happiness as a gift and thank my Higher Power for it.

Boredom

Is not life a hundred times too short
for us to bore ourselves?
—Friedrich Nietzsche

Boredom is a form of conceit. When we are bored we are saying, "Okay, life, you are not doing your job of keeping me entertained." To think that life or those around us or the world itself is here primarily to keep us amused and entertained is "Stinking thinking."

This thinking can screw up our attitude and take us back to the point where our addiction seems like the only way out of that boredom. We may be miserable, but at least we aren't bored, we think.

Those who learn to work the program find that life is far from boring. Each day brings many quiet moments of joy, compassion, and insight. Rich serenity replaces the empty landscape of boredom.

I am not in recovery just to be abstinent;
I am living to learn, to help others, and to
keep busy through positive action.

Relationships

Think for yourselves and let others enjoy the right to do the same.
— *Voltaire*

One of the gifts of recovery is realizing that we can walk away from our prison cells as free people. We are no longer dependent on any other person, place, or thing for our happiness and well-being. The jail of our own making has dissolved. We discover a Power that can provide for every imaginable need.

We realize that the war is over and we have won. We have finally found a way out of our addictions. Morning has broken from our dark night. We listen to other people share their experiences in recovery and realize they are telling our story. Each time we clasp hands, we sense the power of the fellowship running through us. Our sponsors and fellow members keep our eyes focused on recovery.

I am learning to listen enough to hear the truth and speak enough to tell the truth. I am learning not to become overly dependent on others and to avoid having anyone become too dependent on me.

K.I.S.S.

Keep it simple, stupid!
—*Anonymous*

When we were using, our addicted minds were too clever for their own good. They told us lies. They told us that we knew things we didn't, that we were strong when we weren't. The addicted mind tried to analyze recovery and find its fatal flaws. That way it could return to addiction with all the reasons why the program can't and shouldn't work. But the program doesn't have its foundation in this type of reasoning. Its foundation is faith, and faith defies reason. Reason is complicated. Faith is very simple.

Our addictions are clever, baffling, powerful, and very patient. Our program disciplines this addiction with the simple truth. We fight the addiction with honesty. Our program has revealed to us that truth is not complicated. It is simple. We should not dress the truth up in fancy clothes.

I want to keep it simple, just as it is.
I won't use my clever mind to twist the truth.
My program tells me that I need to keep it simple, just as I found it.

Resentments

Nothing on earth consumes a man more completely as the passion of resentment.
—Friedrich Nietzsche

Resentments are among the greatest roadblocks along the route we travel toward a more rewarding way of life. We recognize resentments for what they are: real or imagined grievances against some people, places, and things. They give us an excuse to brood and plan revenge.

Resentments come to all of us at different times. We are only hurting ourselves by holding on to them. It is a waste of time that could be spent enjoying the more positive aspects of our lives.

Our program can teach us how to respond with love, understanding, and compassion to the people, places, and things that displease us. We learn not to fight the windmills of resentment.

Today I'll remember, resentment doesn't hurt others; it only hurts me. Time wasted in getting even can never be used in getting ahead.

True Selves

To thine own self be true.
— William Shakespeare

If we committed suicide within the early years of recovery, we would be killing a stranger. We look back over our hopes, dreams, and ambitions of a few years ago, and they share little or no resemblance with those we have today. When we look at the people in our lives today, we see not only that they're different people—they are entirely different *kinds* of people.

The person who is emerging in our recovery is one we truly like. Where has that person been all our lives? We were too scared to reveal this self to the world. Our ego put it down and called it inadequate, ugly, and good-for-nothing.

Our program has helped us put a lid on our egos and our true self is becoming a wonderful friend. We are no mistake; we are loved by our Higher Power and we are capable of wonderful things.

I do not have to live my life according to the demands of others. I do not have to change my identity to please anything or anyone. It is to myself that I shall be true.

Gifts

You give but little when you give of your possessions. It is when you give of yourself that you truly give.

—Kahlil Gibran

The things that really count in life are not those we can hold in the hand, but those we cherish in the heart. Material possessions can be replaced, at least in part, if they are stolen, lost, or destroyed. But those things that are of greatest value to our security, serenity, and continued growth are safe within our minds and hearts.

Even when we give generously from this store of precious spiritual tools, they magically remain with us to be given away again and again. We are taught to give, share, and be helpful without expecting others to be in our debt.

When I give of myself, the sharing doesn't stop after a single act. Those gifts are passed from one to another to form an endless chain of love.

The Now

Yesterday is gone; forget it. Tomorrow never comes; don't worry. Today is here; get busy.

—Anonymous

When we live in the now, for this day only, "One day at a time," we assure ourselves a comfortable reality. We cannot afford to regret the past. Solutions that worked for yesterday's problems might be obsolete today.

Thinking into the future is projection, an act of purely wishful thinking that is a waste of precious time for growth. The time we spend "projecting" is time wasted. The future is never what we project it to be. Instead of spending time thinking about the future in the present, we can be spending time making the present better.

The only thing that emerges from thinking about the negative parts of our past is guilt and shame. The only thing that emerges from thinking about our future is fear of the unknown. We can eliminate guilt, shame, and fear from our present lives by dealing only with the present.

Today I will spend each moment in the here and now, making the present better.

One Day at a Time

Half our life is spent trying to find something to do with the time we have rushed through life trying to save.

— Will Rogers

Doesn't life sometimes seem like a jigsaw puzzle with all the pieces scattered on the floor? Our program provides us with simple instructions for matching the pieces. We are told if we follow these few instructions, in time we will begin to see the picture develop. But there can be no shortcuts. We can start anywhere, but the picture will only emerge one piece at a time.

Each day for us is like a piece of the jigsaw puzzle. It gives a glimpse of the picture of our lives. We learn that we must live the whole day through to get to the next day. There is no way to get to tomorrow but through today. "One day at a time" becomes the key to the future.

I will only be able to keep my addictions in check today. I can do anything for one day. This is the only day I have, so let me do the best I can.

Emotions

We know too much and feel too little. At least we feel too little of those creative emotions from which a good life springs.

—Bertrand Russell

A fear of dealing with deep emotional experiences must not become a retreat from reality. We can't stick our heads and our hearts in the sand and avoid experiencing our emotions, and still hope to grow in the program. Only robots are emotionless, unable to grow and change.

We need energy to make the spiritual growth to which we aspire. All emotions are sources of energy. None are static. Power emerges from every emotion, be it positive and constructive, or negative and harmful. The power unleashed by our emotions will fuel our spiritual growth if we use it correctly.

We need to steer the energy of dangerous emotions such as fear and anger into beneficial channels. We need to keep emotions like love and humility from becoming excessive.

I am fortunate to have found a way to deal with positive and negative emotions through my recovery program.

Rose Gardens

Give me roses to remember
in the shadow of December.
—Margaret L. Woods

When we began recovery, nobody promised us a rose garden. Yet each day in recovery we find that we do have a rose garden full of cherished beauty.

No flower garden will ever produce lovely blooms for us unless we work constantly at weeding, hoeing, mulching, fertilizing, pruning dead wood, watering, and spraying for plant enemies. How much spiritual growth our garden brings us depends on the amount of spade work we do.

The gifts of the program are realized when we put our best efforts to work. This way of life is based on our positive action.

I must make my life like rich soil
so that what is planted within me
will be nourished and grow.

Service

Whomsoever shall compel you to go with him one mile . . . go with him two. . . . Go another mile.
— Og Mandino

No effort must ever seem so great that it will stop us from giving completely of ourselves in helping someone find the kind of life others helped us find. It is the responsibility of each member to go to any lengths in giving service. Whatever sacrifice it may require from us will bring great rewards.

We always learn that, in the act of one person helping another, no person can give without receiving or get without giving. We learn from our sponsors that when they help us, they are also helping themselves. This experience is a very important part of the program. Our First, Second, and Fifth Traditions are grounded in the principle of service to others. We are privileged to share in that experience.

When I undertake to help another person or our fellowship, I must strive to do more and serve better than is expected of me.

Let Go, Let God

WILLPOWER = Our WILL-ingness to use a HIGHER POWER

—*Anonymous*

One of the greatest decisions any of us ever made concerned our Third Step. This decision seemed to go against everything we wanted to do. We all know so well that every time we tried to manage our own lives, we produced misery and heartache. Human beings seem created to fight the decision to give up control. Yet this decision in Step Three, very hard for us to make, was one of the greatest decisions we ever made.

When we did our Third Step, we merely embraced the truth. When we decided to let God be God, we were able to participate in the plan. Whenever we "Let go and let God," we become a player on a team that will always win.

When what I knew in the past was mostly failure, the decision to let God's will become mine continues to make sense.

Serenity

Give me, kind Heaven, a private station—
a mind serene for contemplation.

—*Alexander Pope*

Serenity must be a permanent state of mind, not a temporary experience. We know that some degree of serenity must be present before acceptance is possible. Acceptance is an ongoing act required for any success in a recovery program. Therefore, it is obvious that we can't afford to settle for merely feeling at peace.

Peace of mind is a mood we can create for ourselves only. Peace leaves as an attitude changes. Serenity is a lifetime possession because it is not only *with* us but also *within* us. It cannot be taken away.

Serenity is positive. It is not a placid or negative state of being. It is a positive force for good.

Today I'll remember serenity comes and lasts when I stay tuned to God's will and the principles of the program.

Love Is . . .

The pleasure of love is in loving.
—François de La Rochefoucauld

Love is one of the most useful tools we have for building a house for spiritual living. We received love generously from new friends in our fellowship who told us "Let us love you until you can learn to love yourself." Today we are happiest when we give love rather than seek it.

Love is being available to anyone who is in need. May we always give love to the seemingly unlovable until we can see them as lovable. Our ultimate joy would be to do each day, one act of love in such a way that nobody but us would ever know its origin.

In recovery, the simplest love we can give is to wish others well. Our worst enemy would never deserve a wish that they resume the bondage of addiction.

Today I'll find love in my Higher Power,
the program, and my friends.

• FEBRUARY 15 •

The Promises

The spiritual life is not a theory. We have to live it.
— Big Book of Alcoholics Anonymous

On page 83 of the Big Book, there begins a long paragraph worthy of study. The sentences in that paragraph have been referred to as "the promises."

We who are finding spiritual growth should frequently take time to examine the promises we find in working our program. We always discover that we are working toward a definite purpose for promised rewards.

Just before the listing of the promises, we read that we will be surprised at the spiritual progress we have made after finishing the Ninth Step. The Ninth Step concerns making direct amends.

We once believed that we needed a certain substance or behavior in order to avoid loneliness and boredom. The promises get rid of that idea. We are made aware that "God wants us to be happy, joyous, and free."

After completing the journey through the first nine Steps, the promises begin to unfold for me.

The First Promise

We will know a new freedom and happiness.
— Big Book of Alcoholics Anonymous

A new freedom and happiness for us is an almost unbelievable promise. Before recovery, we had little choice and less freedom. Everything we did had to be set up to meet the demands of our compulsion. Try as hard as we possibly could, we could never prevent the consuming urge of our addiction. A powerful compulsion took over all our waking hours.

Our lives were controlled by our desires. There was a constant need to bow to the demands of our addiction. It made all our decisions for us. There was no freedom and only a small bit of happiness at the very best. We always had to "pay the piper," and we knew it. We were slaves, like it or not. When freedom came with abstinence, so came joy, gratitude, and love for others and ourselves.

I once believed that I could control my addiction. When I found it wasn't possible, I felt deep depression, guilt, shame, and remorse. I felt I no longer had freedom. Recovery finally gave me a choice. Promises do come true.

The Second Promise

We will not regret the past nor wish to shut the door upon it.

— Big Book of Alcoholics Anonymous

In the program, we begin to "clean house" and "get our acts together." As long as we denied and tried to hide from the world, and ourselves, the truth of what kind of person we were when we were using, there would be no approach to abstinence and little possibility of ever preventing relapse.

Without awareness of what the past did to us, we, even if clean and sober, will find ourselves unable to truly carry the message of hope and the gift of a new life to those who desperately need it. Relating our past experiences builds a common ground of love and service between us and the ones for whose awakening we have declared ourselves responsible. Because of that honesty, newcomers can come to realize that they are not alone and that they, too, can "make it."

My past must be visited but never lived in for long.

The Third Promise

We will comprehend the word serenity and know peace.

—Big Book of Alcoholics Anonymous

When we read this promise, we nod our heads eagerly. When we first decided to shake the bondage of addiction through the love, encouragement, deep concern, and help from newfound friends, we knew what serenity felt like. A life of serenity and security comes naturally when we realize that all those who preceded us in our fellowship have not only had the same problems, but have found solutions that they willingly pass on to us.

Peace of mind is new to us. Serenity becomes refreshing and comfortable as we realize we are free men and women, and come to admit to ourselves that we have experienced a miracle.

With that awareness, we find true belief. With abstinence comes mental clarity. Serenity gives us a perfect climate in which spiritual progress can grow.

I am free to seek that precious peace of mind that can mature within me. I live daily with the familiar Serenity Prayer.

The Fourth Promise

No matter how far down the scale we have gone, we will see how our experience can benefit others.

— Big Book of Alcoholics Anonymous

What excitement comes to us when we discover that we are not useless human beings! When we drank or used, we thought we were doomed to be incompetent, unworthy, and useless persons. No more!

Our escape from the depths of despair makes us feel needed and trusted. Others listen to our stories of how we were, what happened, and what we are today. They cry out, "That's me. I was that way. I did all those same things."

We come to know we deserve that trust, that companionship, that acceptance. We are worthy human beings. We can help others experience miracles. When we tell of our degrading existence with alcohol and drugs, we are useful and important to those who listen. Our negative experiences become positive forces in helping others find the road to recovery.

Recovery brings me the realization that I can become a helpful person by sharing those very experiences that made me feel worthless.

The Fifth Promise

The feeling of uselessness and self-pity will disappear.

—Big Book of Alcoholics Anonymous

When we were deep within the bewilderment and agony of our addiction, we often moaned, "What's the use? Nobody cares." We considered ourselves "lost people." We thought we were incapable of ever doing anything worthwhile for anyone, including ourselves. Shame and guilt made us wallow in self-pity, but we never blamed ourselves. It was always those people, places, and things out there that made us victims.

We complained, "They did it to me. I'm not to blame. If it hadn't been for bad luck . . . I was just in the wrong place at the wrong time."

In recovery, we often refer to self-pity as the P.L.O.M.s (poor little old me). We learn to recognize and avoid the P.L.O.M.s by working our program and by focusing on positive things.

When I surrendered to my addiction, I was always sure I had been betrayed by others. I was sorry for myself. Now the promise has come true. I am useful and free of self-pity.

The Sixth Promise

We shall lose interest in selfish things
and gain interest in our fellows.
— Big Book of Alcoholics Anonymous

We came into the program as experts in dishonesty, deceit, envy, and self-pity. Selfishness was an attitude that fitted us well. We were shameless in the ways we took advantage of other people. The victims of our selfishness most often were those who loved us and tried to help us.

Our self-importance was based on unreality and was the effect of addicted behavior. We engaged in far-out thinking that reached the heights of fantasy. Our self-centeredness and selfishness developed within all of us a sick ego that turned into a powerhouse of grandiosity. The arrogance of an ego-driven addict was a drawback to willingness. In such a state of being, only miracles could help us.

In my addiction, my selfishness made me a "me-first" person. In recovery, I am interested in the well-being of others. This has caused my self-interest to disappear.

• FEBRUARY 22 •

The Seventh Promise

Self-seeking will slip away.
— Big Book of Alcoholics Anonymous

When we were using, constant self-seeking was our whole existence. Being forced to cut down or stop was impossible to imagine. It was an invasion of our right to live as we wished. It didn't matter that our choice was creating physical suffering and mental anguish for us and those who loved us.

We were always on the defensive. Our answer to any accusation or plea to quit was always "it's none of your business," or "let me live my own life."

With abstinence, we began to practice understanding, humility, gratitude, caring and sharing with others, open-mindedness, faith in our program's recovery Steps, love of others, and belonging in a world of positiveness and action. We are beginning to attain a life where we realize we are truly people who need people.

When I became abstinent, I learned that making constant spiritual progress is what life is truly all about, and the self-seeking slipped away.

The Eighth Promise

Our whole attitude and outlook on life will change.

— Big Book of Alcoholics Anonymous

Before the program, the only changes in our lives were in the substances we were using, our companions, or the places we went to use. We only changed the way we obeyed the commands of our compulsion. What didn't change was the fact that our lives always became worse.

We never admitted that our addiction was our enemy. We always considered it to be a friend in times of need. We believed it was the only way to enjoy life—until it began to destroy that life. Then we realized it must be put entirely out of our lives if we were to survive.

Our attitudes and outlook on life changed for the better in every way when we began to practice abstinence and work the Steps.

Today I see exciting changes occurring physically, emotionally, and spiritually. I am no longer a slave to the limited changes dictated by my addiction.

The Ninth Promise

Fear of people and of economic insecurity will leave us.

— *Big Book of Alcoholics Anonymous*

When we were deep in our compulsions and obsessions, we were afraid of people, especially those who loved us. We were terrified we would not have the necessities of life. And we usually lost both.

Addiction so warped our minds we were constantly fantasizing dangers from sources we could not identity or bring into focus. These fantasies became our reality. All the "ghosts that never were" could be traced to one major fear: that of the unknown. We distrusted people, places, and things.

Now we welcome them. Our new friends, surroundings, and tools for living are life-saving. Now when "fear knocks, faith answers—and no one is there." Our program teaches us to trust ourselves, others, and our Higher Power. The rest takes care of itself.

The only things I used to trust were those I was addicted to. When I began to put my trust in the program and my Higher Power, the destruction stopped and recovery began.

The Tenth Promise

We will instinctively know how to handle situations which used to baffle us.
— Big Book of Alcoholics Anonymous

By using such slogans as "Easy does it," "One day at a time," or "Together we can do what I can't," we find solutions for problems that seemed unsolvable before. By working the Steps, we learn to face up to and solve the problems of everyday living that used to cause us to seek relief in our addictions.

We no longer have doubts about our ability to do for ourselves what we once expected others to do for us. If we don't know the answers, we know we can find them by asking the advice of fellow members who have faced the same problems.

The instincts that once compelled us toward our addiction have been redirected toward solving problems during recovery. We are confident that there are solutions to all problems, including some we haven't faced yet. We no longer have to dodge what we used to feel were certain failures.

I use the tools built by those who have already experienced the problems I am facing for the first time.

The Eleventh Promise

We will suddenly realize that God is doing for us what we could not do for ourselves.
— Big Book of Alcoholics Anonymous

When we are new in recovery and survive a major problem or make progress, we try to explain it by saying we have been saved by coincidence. Then our new friends are quick to tell us that there are no coincidences in recovery, only miracles. God is doing for us what we could not do for ourselves.

As we meditate on this promise, we must practice patience, belief, and trust in our Higher Power. God always lets us know that miracles come in His time, not ours.

This promise tells us we must accept God's help, not merely be resigned to it. We must let go of our problems personally and turn them over to God with faith.

When I drank or used, my Higher Power was the substance I was using. I seldom admitted it. The eleventh promise tells me I have found a Higher Power that can and will do great things for me in spite of myself.

The Twelfth Promise

[The promises] will always materialize if we work for them.

— Big Book of Alcoholics Anonymous

Emotional growth and the fulfillment of the promises are not gifts we receive without any effort on our part. We must earn the results by serious, dedicated work. The Steps are the tools we use to do that work.

We can think of progress as a partnership between us and our Higher Power. Directions are given and the promises are made good to us when we follow those directions.

We must first develop complete open-mindedness before we can even start to work the necessary parts of our program. We must develop an attitude of rigorous honesty. Finally, we must rid ourselves of denial, deceit, taking shortcuts, holding on to old ideas, and being satisfied with half-measures. All this must be done before we ever taste the success of the promises made to us.

My meditations bring me to the realization that I must always follow instructions in order to succeed in spiritual matters. God gives directions clearly. Unless I do the footwork, nothing will happen.

Sponsorship

Sponsors: Have one, use one, be one.

—Anonymous

Before we were in the program very long, it was suggested we find a sponsor. We found an individual who had the kind of recovery we wanted. The purpose of finding a sponsor was to have someone who would guide us through the Twelve Steps and help us apply the Steps to problems we encountered.

Sponsorship is one of the important ways of carrying the message. Sponsors share their experience of working the program freely. They do not nag or manage our lives. At times, sponsors may appear to be very strict, but they're only trying to pass on their knowledge. They have a deep concern about our recovery.

The first thing my sponsor said to me was "Get a check-up from the neck up." I followed the advice. I am grateful for all the help my sponsor has given me.

Realities

[R]ealities are less dangerous than fantasies . . . fact-finding is more effective than fault-finding.

—*Carl Lotus Becker*

Accepting reality is a beginning toward progress for recovering addicts. Reality always gives us plain answers, not empty desires. Empty desires are fantasies.

Reality can't be replaced by rationalizing. We can't afford guesswork in seeking answers to how we can achieve serenity and grow in character. We must have the facts.

Reality cannot change, but our attitudes can. What happens to us is not our responsibility, but our reactions to what happens to us are. We spend time trying to become the person we want to be. We no longer spend time finding fault with the person we are.

The program teaches us to work for progress, not perfection. We no longer set ourselves up for failure by trying to be perfect.

Reality warns me not to look for answers in a mirror, but to listen to truth from the heart.

Best Efforts

If I can stop one heart from breaking,
I shall not live in vain.

—Emily Dickinson

Success can't be measured by the number of those who have heard a message of hope for a better life. We constantly remind ourselves of this whenever a single cry for help arises. One success in a Twelve Step group more than makes up for any number of failures.

We can never feel discouraged by delays in success. We keep giving the message since we know that God's delay does not mean God's denial.

When success comes we are reminded not to let pride carry us away. We have learned in recovery to keep our winnings in proper perspective.

I am not in the results business.
My main task is to make my best effort.
Results are added benefits.

Gratitude

We have no right to ask, when sorrow comes, "why did this happen to me?" unless we ask the same question for every joy that comes our way.

—Philip S. Bernstein

Self-pity used to overwhelm us. We bitterly asked why fate had burdened us with the obsession that brought us to a Twelve Step group. Now that recovery fills our lives, we are grateful for the good fortune that we have been shown a way out.

Gratitude brings humility for our progress and compassion for all those who still suffer. We are not only grateful for what we have received. We are grateful for the opportunity to give. We want to always do more than feel grateful. We need to express that gratitude.

My reply to every complaint I have is "compared to what?" No matter how badly I think I hurt today, every day with my old problems was worse.

Self-Esteem

We can help one another find out the meaning of life. But in the last analysis, each is responsible for finding himself.

— Thomas Merton

"Because of my changed attitude, I am today the best me I've ever been." The ability to say those words at any moment is one of the many rewarding experiences of recovery. Those words are not boastful. They describe a newly found self-esteem.

Those words go beyond satisfaction for our ability to correct character defects and make amends. They are more than an appreciation of character growth. They are a daily personal challenge to make every tomorrow a day on which we can repeat the words, "I am the best me ever."

Whatever progress I make will not come to me as a gift. I need to work for every inch of growth. Others can show me the way to be the "best me ever," but I have to do the work.

Facing Problems

If you find a path with no obstacles,
it probably doesn't lead anywhere.
—*Anonymous*

We are constantly aware that problems aren't burdens suffered by us alone. Since the beginning of time, all humanity has had to cope with problems. We need to remember to identify with others and their problems, and not compare our problems to theirs to see who has the greater troubles. This will also eliminate self-pity during crises.

By accepting these difficulties, we can begin at once to seek advice from friends who have solved similar problems. By *walking through* problems without complaint instead of timidly trying to sneak around them, we will grow spiritually.

Problems won't get rid of my character defects;
problems expose them. By facing difficulties
through the program, I will grow spiritually.

Needing People

I was never less alone than when by myself.
—Edward Gibbon

In order to continue to grow spiritually, we will, happily, always be among the lucky people who need people. For the rest of our lives, we will give to friends and receive from them. We will make progress together. But each must welcome the reality that he or she needs, at times, to be alone with only personal thoughts.

Such times fill the necessity for prayer and meditation. We will never be at a loss for inspiration for contemplation. New friends said, "Welcome to our world." We can well meditate on that wonderful world of gratitude, love, honesty, open-mindedness, willingness, and other elements of spiritual progress.

I must be like a ship's captain who constantly consults instruments to make sure I am properly on course. My "instruments" are other people. What they teach me is what feeds my meditations when I am alone. That way I am never alone.

Patience

How poor are they that have not patience.
— William Shakespeare

Patient people do not simply stand and suffer. They are busy carefully planning what positive thing they will do next.

It is simple to start demanding wisdom *right now*. But patience is teamed with acceptance. One doesn't happen without the other. Wisdom comes with acceptance, and that takes patience. We can't demand it. We can only accept it.

Patience does not tell us, "grin and bear it." It does remind us that if we resist acting rashly, all answers *will* come, in God's time, not ours. Patience promises rewards for tomorrow and nourishes a desire for change, if we give progress ample time.

Patience insists that I make real instead of false starts at growth. It tells me that my greatest teacher is time. I must act only when my plans are well constructed.

• MARCH 7 •

Responsibility

Faith is our greatest gift; it's sharing with others, our greatest responsibility.

—*Anonymous*

Places and things never wronged us. We justify old actions when we blame other people for what we once did to ourselves. This can cause us to return to old behaviors.

We want to give up all stinking thinking. We cannot safely act the way we think we are expected to, but we can work at being ourselves.

We take risks only if they aim at spiritual progress. We become assertive only in seeking whatever can help us grow. Above all, we must try to stop being a "blame thrower" and start shouldering our responsibilities. If we react with compassion, understanding, and love, then we will achieve spiritual progress. If we let ourselves be hurt or angry or full of self-pity, we achieve no growth and accept no responsibility.

It's not always what happens that is my responsibility; it's how I react to what happens.

Open Minds

Minds are like parachutes. They won't work unless they are open.

—Anonymous

Unless we maintain open minds, we cannot hope to make attitude changes for the better. Open-mindedness will prevent selfishness and reduce the possibility of painful resentments by not allowing intolerance and prejudice.

It is fortunate that we are individuals with personal opinions and that we can express different views without causing problems. We can disagree without being disagreeable. Besides, variety in viewpoints keeps recovery from being dull or boring.

In our program, open minds remind us that common welfare comes before personal wishes.

When I lock the doors of my mind, I am keeping more of value out of my heart than can ever be harbored in a tightly closed mind.

Procrastination

Procrastination is the art of
keeping up with yesterday.
— Don Marquis

We were constant procrastinators before we began our Twelve Step program. Addiction created the habit of delay because, as long as we had our substance, everything else could wait.

Now we know that action truly is the magic word. The slogan "Easy does it" doesn't mean to put things off. It means to do it, but to do it in God's good time. Slow growth doesn't mean postponement.

We can't put off airing problems to other people for fear of being ridiculed. We need answers early during our progress. When we attempt to ask for solutions, we can be clear and direct in our questions. We know our friends will always give us the right to be wrong and quickly correct faulty thinking.

I can solve problems just by pressing on.
Procrastination is not living one day at a time.
I will do today what I am meant to do today.

Complacency

First we work the program because we HAVE to. Then we work the program because we are WILLING to. Finally we work the program because we WANT to.

—*Anonymous*

To think at any time that our battle for continuous emotional growth has been won could be the biggest mistake in our life today. Self-satisfaction is a tougher enemy than discouragement. Overconfidence can make us open to self-importance and a target for failure.

Watchfulness has to be the guiding force in everyday living. We will always remember that people like us who once lived with despair usually find it more difficult to deal with success than with failure.

We can fight tendencies toward being smug by being alert to it. Watchfulness takes patience.

It would be easy to become complacent if I began to believe that all I had to do in recovery was to accept my problems and relax. As my sponsor says, "If we don't grow, we gotta go."

The Ready Pupil

God gave us two ears but only one mouth. Some say that's because our Higher Power wanted us to spend twice as much time listening as we did talking.

—*Anonymous*

One of the most valuable things we can do is to become a good listener. When we concentrate on absorbing what wiser and more experienced members say, rather than thinking about what we imagine others want to hear from us, we will grow in our program. We are aware that "when the pupil is ready, the teacher will appear."

Often, the teacher is an unlikely source. Some of the things we most need to hear may come from someone new to the program. If we are highly educated, it may come from someone with no education at all. If we are materially successful, it may come from someone who has nothing. We are all teachers and all students in the program. We constantly learn from each other, wherever or whoever we are.

I shall never stop learning as I will always be a pupil in my program. Thankfully, I will never graduate. There are no diplomas, only revelations. I will be a good listener.

Truth

If you don't tell the truth about yourself,
you cannot tell it about other people.
— Virginia Woolf

Truth, like all precious things, can be both given and accepted joyously. But we will give it only after much examination of our motives and the possible effect on the person who receives it. Hastily offered truth can be more harmful than silence.

If truth can motivate either healing or growth in a friend, we can't hesitate to speak it, even if it makes us uncomfortable. May we also gratefully accept truths about ourselves from others. We will know they are offered as gifts. We shall always try to speak the truth with love. Love and truth complement each other. Love without truth is sentimentality; truth without love is cruelty.

I will be careful when I speak the truth,
trying to be helpful and not hurtful to others.

Willingness

God is not willing to do everything and thus take away our free will and the share of glory which belongs to us.

—*Niccolò Machiavelli*

To be willing is to be ready and prepared. If we are willing, we are eager to accept even unfamiliar challenges if those challenges promise rewarding results.

Willingness is not to be confused with being willful. Willfulness can return us to our old habits of wanting everything our way and on our own terms. Willingness prepares us to accept responsibilities. It gives us courage to change our attitudes. It rids us of fears of living in an imperfect world.

We have become willing to practice the principles of the program, willing to continue our spiritual progress, and willing to work at our new way of life.

I can always profit by being strong-willed, as long as that means "strong-willingness," not hardheadedness.

Backing Off

He has spent all his life letting down baskets into empty wells.

—Sydney Smith

We can always resist an argument where there is obviously no chance of either side solving a problem. Taking time to evaluate the situation will save us possible embarrassment and apologies.

We don't have to be winners in matters that are unimportant to spiritual progress. We have also learned that there is no disgrace in changing directions when one way won't work.

Of course, nobody wins by retreating from a confrontation, but aggressiveness is sure to be useless. Sometimes backing off *is* winning if nothing is to be gained by confrontation. We can often avoid another blow to the wounded dignity we brought into our program.

To avoid what is impossible to win doesn't make me a quitter.

Solitude

I never found the companion that
was so companionable as solitude.
—Henry David Thoreau

Before the activities of any day begin, we dress our minds as carefully as we dress our bodies. Each day requires both planning and examining if it is to be helpful in our spiritual Twelve Step progress. We perform such duties in solitude. Otherwise we will be lacking in the ability to cope and get the best from each day.

At the end of the day, silent and alone in thought, we weigh our words and actions of the past hours so we may understand how well we measured up to the hopes and expectations we had at the day's beginning. That way, we can enrich tomorrow's plans by the successes or mistakes we uncover.

Daydreams are not worthless if I have hopes
they can come true and faith that they will
materialize. Solitude is my companion
when I plan and evaluate.

Attending Meetings

Three suggestions for speaking at meetings: be interesting, be brief, be seated.

—*Anonymous*

The meetings we attend are like stones for the foundation of recovery. Some meetings we give more than we take; others, we take away more than we give. We always win either way. We remember that when we are called on to speak, we are but a fellow traveler. What makes us unique are not our pretty faces, interesting voices, or important jobs. It is our story, the exact way we are experiencing our recovery.

Our lives are much more interesting than our opinions. When we share our actual experiences, people take much more away than if we just share an idea. We are normally long-winded with an opinion and short-winded with an actual illustration. When we address a group we are humble. It is only by the grace of God that we are asked to share with the group.

At meetings I will share my recovery experiences and not my opinions.

• MARCH 17 •

This Too Shall Pass

Serenity is not freedom from the storm,
but peace during a storm.

—*Anonymous*

We learn in our recovery that life has a way of recreating itself. This discovery is one we are taught not to fight. We remember how badly we hurt when things would pass away from us, whether it was a lost doll, a lost dog, or a lost dad. We closed ourselves off from the possibility that anything of value could come from the loss. Yet the doll was replaced, a cat came into our lives, and a father figure emerged.

The key to staying on our program is to remember that life does recreate itself. There will be many moments when we find ourselves squarely in the middle of a passing away. We will be hurt and wonder how we go on.

Not to worry, this too shall pass. This cold winter of a moment will break soon into a sunny spring of a future.

There can be no comings if there are no goings. Life can't be recreated if there is no passing away. I need to remember that sometimes it is darkest before daybreak.

Learning

I have learned . . . tolerance from the intolerant and kindness from the unkind. I should not be ungrateful to these teachers.

— Kahlil Gibran

Once again, we are students. This time we are learning the secrets of living completely. These secrets have always been around us. We only had to clear our thinking of the obsessions, dependencies, denials, excessiveness, fears, jealousies, and other destructive ideas and habits that ruled us. We had to open our minds to accept and our hearts to understand.

We have found teachers in our program. Each teacher is a new friend. We learn from them, and they learn from the growth of our awareness: We find lessons in the glaring faults we see in others. We learn from our own errors.

In my troubled years, I remembered my school days as perhaps the happiest of my life. I thought they were gone forever. But I've found them again in the program, and I love being back in school.

Laughter

The most useless day of all is that
in which we have not laughed.
—Sebastien R.N. Chamfort

When we wallowed in the self-pity of obsession, we were sure we'd never laugh again. How easy it was to weep, alone and secretly, inspired by sad music like "Born to Lose" or "I'm So Lonesome I Could Cry."

What a shock it was to hear people laugh in our first few meetings! How could they laugh about something as serious as addiction? What an awakening when we were able to join the laughter!

We laughed with them as they laughed at the sad objects they once were. Today we can also laugh for pure joy at being free of restraints, and in gratitude for the resolve not to return to our old ways. We can laugh just for being alive.

Laughter is a source of growth for me.
It keeps me thinking positively. It reduces
the stress of problems. It tells me that
any effort at progress is worthwhile.
Laughter is progress.

Act as If . . .

In the arena of human life the honours and rewards fall to those who show their good qualities in action.

—*Aristotle*

The only way to get what we need is to "Act as if" we have it. The key word for us is *act.*

We have discovered that knowledge often follows action rather than vice versa. When we *fake it* in our early days, we find ourselves *making it* in later days.

In the beginning, we are asked to "Act as if" we are following instructions, trusting the program, listening to sponsors, and coming to believe. The amazing thing is that soon we *were* doing those very things.

We were never able to think our way into recovery. Our minds created a tremendous amount of trouble for us. We needed to turn our minds down (not off). We soon discovered the difference between doing and thinking.

The key to "Acting as if" is faith. With faith, the promises will come true for me. The way to faith is through my fears. I turn fears over to my faith and simply "Act as if."

Friendship

The only reward for virtue, the only way to have a friend is to be one.

—Ralph Waldo Emerson

Friendship is not a one-word motto to be hung on a wall. Friends are not statues to decorate a mantle. Friendships are as real to us as love and gratitude, and friends are as much a part of all our lives as the air we breathe.

Without friends, we could not enjoy the full benefits of recovery. All the truths we follow daily we receive from friends through hearing or reading their messages but mostly by watching them in action. Our primary goal is to add to our wisdom by giving. Without friendships, our caring and sharing would be empty gestures.

None of us needs ever to be alone again because each of us in our own way works for the good of others. We are bound together by a common problem and work together on the solution.

If I permit myself to become incapable of friendship, I will find that I will be unable to reveal myself to others and to my inner self.

Being Needed

The most general survey shows us that the two foes of human happiness are pain and boredom.

—Arthur Schopenhauer

Filling a need is more vital than being loved. When we are needed, we are automatically loved. No effort of ours can ever be too great or too small.

We have never heard anyone who is involved in a program of spiritual growth complain of being bored. The discoveries and excitement of spiritual exploration are limitless. Also, carrying a message of hope to those who still suffer strengthens our own hold on the serenity and security of a personal recovery.

Feeling needed is the greatest encouragement we will ever receive that our goals can be achievable.

If people stopped volunteering to fill other people's needs, the end of civilization would be close behind. My pain is forgotten and my boredom is gone when I am needed.

Moderation

Stay RIGHT SIZE!
—*Anonymous*

Today our target for a proper living pace is moderation. We know how easy it is to magnify, exaggerate, accent, and overindulge. The dependency and compulsion from which we are steadily recovering puts us among the world's excessive people. Every day we need to tell ourselves that more is not necessarily better.

We also need to guard against unrestraint, greed, and envy. But we can adapt even dangerous instincts like fear and anger into self-improving assets if we can maintain moderation.

In our desire for perfection, however, we also need to practice moderation. We can't want more than we are capable of achieving. We could destroy ourselves by trying to be perfect. In this, above all else, we need to practice moderation, for we will never be perfect.

When I create impossible dreams, they backfire
and blow up and leave me with negative feelings.
I want to practice moderation in all things,
even the good things in life.

Peace

Peace is when time doesn't matter
as it passes by.

—*Maria Schell*

We came into the program with very little peace in our lives. Somebody or something was always coming by and tipping over our apple cart. Everywhere we turned we found nothing but turmoil. All our relationships seemed loaded with pain and anxiety. There were days we cursed God for bringing such chaos into our lives.

The Steps have revealed that we have been the author of turmoil. We have seen how our addiction created war with everything it touched. The energy was within us, and it could not be satisfied until it destroyed everything, including our own lives. The Steps have slain the dragon, quieted the turmoil, won the war. There is now a gentle quality to our relationships, and the attitude of "Live and let live" prevails in our lives.

The need to turn my apple cart over to generate excitement has become a memory. I have finally found my sought-for peace of mind.

One Day at a Time

Time ripens all things. No man's born wise.
—Miguel de Cervantes

We come to understand time in a different way. Each day we discover that there is an order to life that is only revealed day-to-day. The moments when life forces us to reconsider our schedule are no longer met with anger and frustration. We begin to trust our Higher Power to actually dictate what will happen in our lives. We find ourselves staying close to people who have developed some measure of humility for they seem to have a better sense of timing.

We remember the times when we demanded, "I want what I want when I want it." The funny thing was, we were usually disappointed when we got what we wanted.

We are even finding a new appreciation for the seasons of the year and for our lives. We find ourselves enjoying winter just as much as summer, our old age as much as our youth. Each new day deposits within us new wisdom.

Today I will remember that rather than fighting time, I will become time's passenger.

Choices

Use wisely your power of choice.
— Og Mandino

Escape from physical, emotional, and mental control of our old obsessions and dependencies has given all of us the freedom to make choices. But the right to choose is only an opening. We need to exercise that right and to choose well.

We learn that we cannot misuse or neglect choices once we have determined a course to take. We come to know how to choose between positive and negative, humility and arrogance, gratitude and self-centeredness, pride and dejection, high and low spirits. Knowing is not enough, however. We carry out our choices and use wisely the power of choice.

As we work our program, we find that the fear of making decisions slips away. If our choice proves wrong, we can learn from the experience.

I am the result of any choice. I am,
at any given moment of life, the sum total
of the choices I have made.

Forgiving

Joy to forgive and joy to be forgiven
hang level in the balances of love.
—*Richard Garnett*

If we are unable or unwilling to forgive others for whatever they do, we won't be able to forgive ourselves for our actions. The agony of resentment, guilt, remorse, and shame will overpower us. These emotions will halt our progress toward the comfortable and rewarding living we are promised in recovery.

Early in recovery, we often were told to pray for those whom we thought had wronged us. This philosophy is as old as civilization. Forgiveness will always triumph over guilt and shame. Recovery is one-third love and two-thirds forgiveness.

We've been our own worst enemies during most of our lives. We've often hurt ourselves over what we thought was justifiable anger and resentment.

Self-forgiveness is strength not weakness.
Gaining the strength is simple. I need only
remind myself that "God has forgiven me.
Why not forgive myself?"

Ego

E.G.O. = Edge God Out.
—Anonymous

Ego can be one tough customer. It generally fights this business of recovery and a Higher Power tooth and nail. It can cry like a baby and tell us how much care it needs. It can scream like a pouting teenager demanding that we leave it alone. It can romance us like a long-lost lover seducing us into sleep.

The ego can take on many disguises to get its own way. It wants no competition for affection. When we were caught up in our disease, the ego and the drugs and alcohol met up and made an unholy alliance against us. The disease told the ego what it wanted to hear, and the ego fed the disease its poison.

My ego must be cut down to size. This will help stop my disease from doing further damage to my life. My ego will never provide serenity, only endless demand. Only my Higher Power, the program, and my friends can end this war within me.

Togetherness

Nothing that is worth doing can be done alone, but has to be done with others.
— Dr. Reinhold Niebuhr

Countless troubled people have agonized and sometimes died, many by their own hand, because they were defeated loners. They never learned that they needed help in solving what seemed like overpowering problems. It's not a sign of weakness to ask for help. It's a sign of strength.

The more closely we identify with others today, the more certain we are that nobody can solve our problems for us. But caring friends can guide us by sharing their experiences. The secret behind the magical success of sharing is that sharing cannot be done without caring. To care is to experience the most vital part of love.

Sharing problems is only a small part of giving. We must share strengths, successes, experiences, and hopes.

Whenever I am practicing the principles of my program, I am comforted by knowing that I never walk alone. Sometimes, I am led. At other times, I can show the way.

Worst Enemy

Self is the only prison that can
ever bind the soul.
—*Robert Graham*

We refuse to keep putting ourselves down. Sometimes that seems like a virtue, but it isn't. It's a defect. The honest approach is to know our strengths *and* our weaknesses. The program provides us the tools to work on both.

In recovery, each of us chooses to become our own best friend. Liking ourselves will assure us that we can become the best person we can be. Who have we hurt more than we have hurt ourselves? Would we let anyone do to us what we have done to ourselves?

We are learning to think about our assets rather than focusing on our liabilities. Our self-talk no longer always puts us down.

I can strike a solid blow at "me, my worst enemy," by concentrating on the small triumphs of each today rather than on yesterday's disasters.

"Almost" People

If a man has a talent and cannot use it, he has failed. If he has a talent and uses only half of it, he has partly failed.

—Thomas Wolfe

Every step of progress that we make in our program takes us farther away from being one of the "almost" people. We know today that we cannot settle for "almost" living up to our potentials and capabilities.

We used to think that near-misses meant coming close to victory. This was satisfying, we thought. But we actually were making sure our efforts always got worse, never better.

In recovery, we see the wisdom of "half-measures availing us nothing." Today when we miss, we learn from a "near success" and try again, harder.

Even the slogan "Easy does it" can encourage me to see worth in almost-good efforts, but I must quickly add to that "But DO it!"

Humor

Rule 62: Don't take yourself too seriously.
—*Anonymous*

Once we get the God problem figured out, it's easier to lighten up on ourselves. When we play God, we're serious about ourselves because, after all, we're God and God is serious. Besides, carrying the world around on our backs is heavy stuff, and it's hard to laugh when we're so weighted down.

Once we work our Steps, we see things from a clearer point of view. We get a sense of humor back. The slogan "Easy does it" speaks to us.

We watch the old-timers and how they handle situations. There is usually little fuss or hassle. They don't frown or look worried. Those who have been on the program for a long time know that things come and go; God's will *will* be done. Life has a lot more to do with acceptance than with being serious.

Let me learn to accept that God's in charge.
Then I can stop taking myself so seriously.

Dedication

We can act ourselves into right thinking easier than we can think ourselves into right acting.

—Anonymous

The best thing for us to do in our Twelve Step program is to be honest in how we act and think. We must be true to that belief.

We can't think for others, and they can't think for us. Friends can tell us the lessons they have learned from their experiences. If those lessons fit us, we can use them to help guide us and our thinking. We often hear, "Take what you need and leave the rest."

As good for us as our ideas are, we must not force them on others. We can only offer them. And we won't be true to ourselves if we are jealous of other people's ideas. We never know what we can do until we try, and we can't be sure what ideas are best for us until we test them.

Am I dedicated to the beliefs that are best for me in my recovery?

Sticking to It

I shot an arrow into the air. It fell to earth,
I knew not where.

—Henry Wadsworth Longfellow

When we're working hard on something, and we're not sure how it's going to turn out, we sometimes feel hopeless. But we never let that hopeless feeling make us unsure of our goals. As long as we keep trying to help ourselves or others, we can't fail.

Friends always tell us to look past our goals because we can't tell when or where our message will find its mark. We tell ourselves every day that there is no shame in falling down. The shame comes when we fall and don't get up again to make another try. Our strength doesn't come from winning easily.

Our strength comes from winning over hopelessness. If we quit today, tomorrow will be impossible.

May I be strong and stick to my efforts
at personal and spiritual progress.

Slippery Places

If you sit in the barber chair long enough,
you're bound to get your hair cut.

—*Anonymous*

In recovery, we stay aware and keep in contact with our Higher Power. We keep our addictions in check with our Step work. We now know the difference between what is right and wrong for us. We know we are weak and powerless over our addictions. We know it is only by the grace of our Higher Power that we can keep ourselves clean and sober.

So we learn to stay away from slippery places and slippery people. We know we are always just one step away from relapse. We have learned how our wills, uncontrolled, will always look for shortcuts to happiness. When our contact with our Higher Power is weak, we begin to listen to the voices that call us back into the dark days before the program. Our minds play tricks on us. They only let us remember the true and beautiful moments, not the dark and ugly days and nights before the program.

I will stay clear of slippery people and places.

Intolerance

I'm slipping when I accept certain faults in myself, but I don't accept them in other people.

—Anonymous

Our fellowship can pull good deeds out of people who have normally acted badly. Our Steps suggest ways to greatly change our behavior.

We are careful to separate what we say we are *going* to do and what we *actually* do. When we go to meetings and start talking about what wonderful things we are going to do rather than sharing what we have already done, we roll up our sleeves and get to work, because we have a lot to learn. Our friends and sponsor can suggest ways of getting started.

The fellowship doesn't want to hear sermons or judgments on past behavior. That's what happens when we judge ourselves and others, and talk about how we're going to change everybody and everything. We can't just "Talk the talk." We need to "Walk the walk."

I don't want to judge anybody, including myself. Let me learn to be forgiving and tolerant.

Character

Character is what you are in the dark.
—Dwight L. Moody

We're not born with character. We have to build it through patience, self-esteem, and humility. Character is never revealed by what we think or say, no matter how wise our thoughts or our words may be sometimes. Character is what we are underneath all the layers of our defenses that we show the world.

Character is an outer show of an inner glow that reaches others or pleases ourselves. It is a reserve force for all of us. Its usefulness goes beyond talent. Its greatest energy comes from personal relations with others.

Character permits us to welcome healthy criticism. It is a force that respects truth and develops will and spirit. It is positive. It stresses action and makes all of these qualities clear to others.

Let me examine my character and develop it with patience, self-esteem, and humility.

Sexuality

Our sex powers were God-given and therefore good, neither to be used lightly or selfishly nor to be despised and loathed.

—*Big Book of Alcoholics Anonymous*

What comes from our Higher Power is to be honored and treated with respect. Our sexuality has unlimited potential for good. We have so often turned this power in on ourselves and been destroyed by it, or allowed it to destroy others.

The Steps let us change our feelings about sex so that these new feelings can encourage wholesome relationships. When we walk with our Higher Power, our self-will doesn't run riot over our sex lives. Our spiritual awakening washes over all our relationships, even our most tender and personal.

We gain a new sense of respect. We learn we can love deeply. We find that sexuality is a powerful, life-giving force that enriches, bonds, and commits us to a special person. We no longer have to face remorse and guilt from uncontrolled desires.

May I rediscover the joy in my God-given sexuality by treating myself and others with honor and respect.

Wisdom

He who would distinguish the true from the false must have an adequate idea of what is true and false.

—Baruch Spinoza

Wisdom is common sense. It will help us make the right choices in our attitudes and behavior. That way we can continue our spiritual progress.

Sometimes, wisdom is simply willingness to accept with faith the things we don't know from personal experience. We must receive, with an open mind, the messages of those who have lived through the problems we are facing for the first time.

We need to look for and listen to the wisdom in others. If we do, we will gain confidence in our own ability to tell the true from the false. We will begin to practice the principles of our recovery program in all parts of our lives.

Wisdom is earned. Wisdom is precious.
The wise need simply to stand in silence
for their wisdom to reveal itself.
Let me learn wisdom.

• APRIL 9 •

Serving

Serenity or peace of mind is accomplished by very few people in the world. True happiness will come to the person who seeks and finds how to serve others.

—*Anonymous*

We are overjoyed that our giving and sharing is called volunteering. If, in carrying the message of hope, we are volunteers, we are happy to be among those who are volunteers in its purest form. We welcome a chance to serve.

There are no honor rolls, awards, money, or trophies. We give for the pure joy of helping. Our greatest rewards come in the form of a firm handshake or a hug from someone to whom we've given. Sometimes it's the gratitude in the eyes of a family member. That is enough.

I want to practice the advice not to seek glory for kindnesses I perform. I can never be happy if I depend on material rewards for what I have given.

Guilt and Worry

With the Past, as past, I have nothing to do; nor with the Future as future. I live now.
—Ralph Waldo Emerson

We discover a truth about the past and future in our recovery. They are areas over which we have no control, so it's useless to feel guilty about the past or worry over the future. Our Steps have allowed us to clean the slate and make amends for the mess of the past. We receive a generous and loving forgiveness from our Higher Power.

We ask our Higher Power to accept our past mistakes and to free us from the garbage those mistakes have produced. The future is in God's hands. There is nothing we can do about what might happen except to pray for acceptance of God's will. These prayers produce plenty of work for the present. When the future comes, we will be ready.

The amount of time I spend right now feeling guilty or being worried only uses time that I could spend thanking God for the moment I am living. Gratitude will always make mincemeat out of guilt and worry.

Beauty

Beauty as we feel it is something indescribable; what it is or what it means can never be said.
— George Santayana

Beauty is among our most useful and most used words as we progress toward spiritual goals. The kind of beauty that guides our thinking in recovery does not lie on the outside, but rises from within. When we learn to see that beauty in the words, actions, and attitudes of others as well as in the principles we follow, we are choosing well.

Our friends have beauty because of who they really are, not what they may appear to be. The emotions we feel and the living guides we follow are beautiful simply because we need them.

I will have no trouble finding spiritual beauty in our program. True beauty never dies. It is found in all thoughts, attitudes, and emotions, if only I seek it.

Values

By accepting God's help we learn to think clearly, to play fairly, and to give generously.

—Bill P. & Fred H.

Our values change in recovery as we become less and less selfish. The value screen through which we see life is changed. We no longer ask what everyone can do for us; we ask what we can do for them. We no longer seek out situations that only comfort us; we discover ways to comfort. We find that we feel better about ourselves when we help others. We learn from our program that what we have been searching for our whole lives is wrapped up in service to others.

The valuable relationship is the one that creates a closer contact with our Higher Power, so we seek out situations and people that bring us into closer contact.

The values we show in the work of recovery look different from the ones we once held. Every day brings a new chance to become a conductor of life.

My values no longer change with every passing fancy. My life is beginning to mean something and to count for things that are good.

Courage

God, help me to remember that nothing is going to happen to me today that You and I together can't handle.

—*Anonymous*

Courage is what makes us do the right thing even when nobody else is doing it. We can find happiness while surrounded by darkness; we can be loving in the middle of hate and envy, and serene when surrounded by chaos, fear, and anger.

The principles of our program help us face impossible odds. We learn that any act of courage may produce future victory for ourselves and others. The courage that we want takes its strength from faith, not from bravery or physical strength.

Foolish, unthinking courage, though, can be destructive to us or to others. Sensible courage never fails because it is made up of truth and faith.

Let truth and faith give me courage,
so that when fear knocks, no one is there.

Fear

F.E.A.R. = Frustration, Ego,
Anxiety, and Resentment

—*Anonymous*

We don't want to return to the life we led before recovery, but fear should never be the reason why we don't. Fear keeps us from being open to the program. If we're only in the program because we're afraid of the old way of life, we'll never pay attention and open our souls to learn about the new. We'll be too busy looking back over our shoulders to make sure the old life isn't creeping up on us.

We have to want the program out of a desire for a new life, not out of a fear of the old. Positive thinking and behavior will be in charge if we are to make any character growth. Every fear encourages negative thinking that can destroy us. Guilt and shame come from the past, just like fear. If those feelings are what drive us, we will never grow.

I will make it a practice to take note of my fears.
I will take an inventory of each fear until
I understand what caused it. Then I will be able
to find a way to work through them.

Lessons from Pain

The will of God will never take you where
the grace of God will not protect you.
—Anonymous

Today we are living free from compulsions and addictions, but that happiness won't ever let us forget the times we cried from pain. We went through a lot of suffering in order to surrender. All that suffering wouldn't matter if we hadn't become willing to make a spiritual change. We learned valuable lessons from the pain.

In recovery, we learn that pain changes our lives. We gain an understanding of honest values from our suffering. Until we stopped hurting, we couldn't make progress toward a richer life and appreciate the gift of love and service.

I have learned that happiness is getting away
from suffering. Even to crave happiness is painful.
Finding happiness helps me get rid of pain
and find peace of mind.

Seize the Day!

Possibilities and miracles
are one and the same.
—Anonymous

Many of us have seen happiness as a goal we couldn't find. When we were children, we were taught that "life is a hard row to hoe." We carried that over into our adult lives.

Seize the day! We let too many of our days just slide by. None of those hours can be replaced. Why worry over past failures if there is a victory to win? Why keep thinking about our faults when we could be practicing virtues instead?

Seize the day! Hold each moment tight and look at each one with wide-open eyes and mind. They are our lives, special to each of us. The moments pass swiftly into memory. Let those memories be good ones filled with joys large and small.

Yesterday's unhappiness can't be
changed, but today's happiness
is my own responsibility.

Senses

How good is man's life, the mere living!
How fit to employ all the heart and the
soul and the senses forever in joy!
—*Robert Browning*

Our senses are opened up and deepened in our recovery. We see, hear, smell, taste, and touch more strongly. We understand better. There is a beauty to life we could not see before.

We see order where once there was only confusion. We hear music where once there was only noise. We taste sweetness where once there was only bitterness. We smell freshness where once all was stale. We feel softness where once all was rough.

We seem to have changed into a higher form as a result of our Step work. We no longer feel like a wild animal caught in a hunter's trap. We act more and more like human beings. We have an awareness of life that makes us capable of being creative.

I have come to see that the Twelve Steps
are about the recovery of my whole person.

Second Lives

We are here to add what we can to,
not get what we can from, life.
— Sir William Osler

Many of us used to moan, "I wish I were dead." Our addictions and obsessions made us hate ourselves. Other people scorned and pitied us. We wanted to die. We hoped that a life after death would give us rest from our constant battle with compulsions. But today we can find a better answer.

There is life *before* death. Those of us who once cried out, "nobody cares" have found loving, caring friends who share our problems and help us find the answers. They guide us daily through wonderful adventures in living. We all receive great truths in recovery.

I have been given the chance to live two lives.
The cruel one has gone. The second one is
rich with blessings. Nothing must tempt me
to return to the old.

H.A.L.T.

H.A.L.T. = Don't get too hungry or too angry or too lonely or too tired.

—Anonymous

The fellowship has seen many men and women recover from very low and terrible bottoms. When the Steps are carefully worked, miracles can be expected. The lessons aren't hard to understand. The signposts to a relapse are well marked. We can learn a lot from people who have fallen away from the program.

Don't get too hungry. When we are weak physically, it affects our spiritual life. When hungry, eat. We need to stay away from anger altogether. Anger is the breeder of resentments. We have been eaten alive by our grudges. Cool off. Loneliness makes us an easy mark for the many voices that tempt us away from our program. When we feel loneliness coming on, we go to a meeting or use the phone. When we become tired, it is easy for us to remember the substance-induced pick-me-ups we relied on. When we're tired, we need to rest.

Let me remember to eat the right foods, stay calm, use the fellowship, and rest.

Sincerity

The more we love our friends, the less we flatter them; it is by excusing nothing that pure love shows itself.

—*Molière*

The concern we display for those new to our program must always be sincere and honest. When beginners ask for advice, our answer mustn't be phony, but we also need to soften the blow by "truth with love." We can do this by promising them that life will get better if they really want spiritual growth and if they are freely willing to change their attitudes.

If we con anyone with false promises because we don't want to hurt their feelings, they will become our enemy when they find out the truth. This will surely happen when their recovery becomes secure.

If someone in the fellowship makes me angry by telling me a truth that brings me progress, let me be sincere enough to tell them I am grateful.

Earning Rewards

I got a religion that wants to take heaven out of the clouds and plant it right here on earth where most of us can get a slice of it.

— Irwin Shaw

We learn that there are no free trips to abstinence. There aren't any "rain checks" we can take that will give us a head start back to abstinence if we slip. We can't argue that bad luck or betrayal by others were responsible for the relapse.

We won't ever be promised that we will have overnight comfort or success. Our success in the program is decided by how hard we work it. We will get from the Steps only as much as we give. Our investment in serenity and security will earn simple, real interest. There aren't any easy contests to win.

The rewards I receive from the program will be equal to the effort I put into my recovery.

Avoiding Gossip

Tale-bearers are as bad as the tale-makers.
—Richard Sheridan

What we talk about, not *whom* we talk about, is one of the ways we place principle above personalities and practice our Twelfth Tradition. At meetings and over coffee, it's tempting to pass along things we hear about other people who share our recovery.

Before we gossip or find fault with others, wise members teach us to ask ourselves three questions: "Is it true? Is it kind? Is telling it important to help someone's recovery?" If we can't say yes to each question, we mustn't repeat it. If a single word from us hurts someone else, our guilt could throw us back into addiction. Our gossip could cause someone else to lose faith in the program, and throw *them* back into addiction.

I will not gossip. Let me talk about principles, not personalities.

Serenity

Cheerfulness keeps up a kind of daylight in the mind, and fills it with a steady and perpetual serenity.

—Joseph Addison

Our program allows us to stand back from day-to-day confusion and let serenity come into our lives. Our program doesn't take away all the struggle and problems from life, but it does let us learn a different outlook and attitude.

We don't have to get caught up in every storm that blows our way. We don't have to live the pain of every person who crosses our path. We don't have to right every wrong.

Our recovery is a gift to us from a Power greater than we are. We become more and more aware of the meaning of the words in the Serenity Prayer: "God grant me Serenity to accept the things I cannot change, Courage to change the things I can, and Wisdom to know the difference."

Let me learn to see the world as it actually is, not as I want it to be. I trust that my Higher Power didn't make a mistake in designing this world or the plans for my life.

Family

The family is the association established by nature for the supply of man's everyday wants.

—Aristotle

The bond between us and our families becomes tighter in recovery. It's not because they understand or appreciate us more. It's because we understand and appreciate them more. We come to grips with our personal history in our Fourth and Fifth Steps. We are given a clearer point of view on all our relationships. We take more responsibility for what happens to our families, because we learn that we are more than just guiltless victims.

Our Eighth and Ninth Steps let us admit our part in family relationships and mend fences that have been torn down. Our family bonds become tighter because we know we're forgiven. We ask to share that forgiveness with our loved ones.

All of us in our families are loved by our Higher Powers. I don't regret the fact that I can't change the past. I rejoice that the future is open.

Don't Project

What we anticipate seldom occurs. What we least expected generally happens.

— Benjamin Disraeli

We are not in the business of getting results. It's easy and simple to plan results. It's not so easy to just plan and not expect results.

When we think a plan of ours will bring us and humanity all sorts of payoffs, we are playing God again. When our plan doesn't turn out the way we expected, we put ourselves in danger of feeling hopeless. This can lead to relapse.

We remember the past only for what its lessons have taught us about living today. If yesterday was spent in planning how today was supposed to turn out, we will usually be disappointed in today. Today hardly ever turns out the way we had planned or expected it to turn out.

My plans for the future must stay hopes and possibilities. No matter how far I fall short of my plans I must accept the results with serenity. I will work at making plans, but I won't plan the results.

Action

Willingness without action is fantasy.
—Anonymous

The best way to get ready for action is to pray. Prayer makes us ready for success. Sometimes our prayers tell us to go right or go left. Sometimes they just tell us to stand still and wait for orders.

When we are willing to pray, we are willing to act. When we are willing, we are filled with prayer. Prayer always comes before an action.

When we see those who admit they are willing to act but don't lift a finger to help themselves, we don't know what to think. Maybe they are still in the watching phase. Maybe the instructions aren't clear. Or maybe they just haven't prayed.

When I see anyone who is not growing, I will encourage them to pray, attend meetings, and work twice as hard on their Step work.

Hope

Even now I am full of hope,
but the end lies in God.

—*Pindar*

There are many gifts for us in recovery, but no gift is as wonderful as hope. Before we took our First and Second Steps, hope was nothing more than a dream. We hoped for experiences we shouldn't have. All our hoping did was drive a wedge between ourselves and the real world. Our Steps have helped us see that when we stray from the real world, we stray from our Higher Power.

Each Step draws us closer to claiming the promises available to everyone in recovery. If what we hope for is the will of our Higher Power, it will happen. When we hope for a life in recovery, our hope becomes the will of our Higher Power. Then we receive exactly what we need when we need it.

The hope I have is knowing that my
Higher Power will do for me what
I couldn't do for myself.

Anonymity

Anonymity is so important,
it is half our name.
—Anonymous

The Twelfth Tradition of our fellowship states clearly the value we place on our anonymity. It is so important that it becomes part of our identity. We have found the secret to making the many into one. We have discovered the key to fellowship. This Tradition cuts across all the ways we try to separate ourselves from each other.

There is no amount of money, no special title, no circumstance that can break anonymity. We are joined by the one thing we have common: our disease.

Even though we're anonymous, we're still members of the most exclusive club in the world. The only requirement is that we have a problem and a sincere desire to solve it. Our program reminds us that when we attend meetings, we let "who we see there, what we hear there," stay there when we leave.

My anonymous membership in this special club lets me live a life of many rewards.

Those Who Listen

When you do all the talking, you only learn what you already know.

—Anonymous

One of the secrets for finding answers to any emotional problem is to talk with fellow members we can confide in fully. We don't need to look any farther than our sponsor or the members who are part of our recovery. We quickly find those who always hear with a complete understanding about how we feel.

Such friends are perfect listeners because they have suffered and survived the same types of problems. They are compassionate and sympathetic. They listen to us patiently while we completely describe our emotions. Only then do they share details about how they survived. Just knowing that they understand is comforting to us.

My listeners can't solve my problems for me. But they do show how they used the tools that are available in the program to work through the same kinds of problems.

Avoiding Anxiety

Entertaining hope means recognizing fear.
—Robert Browning

We are taught early in recovery not to be afraid of anxiety. It is a normal part of all lives. It can't be stopped or gotten rid of.

We can only deal with anxiety by facing it. It is a vital life force that alerts us that something is wrong with our living patterns. As we act and react to anxiety, we build an ability for thinking through solutions carefully rather than making snap judgments. That way, anxiety helps us learn that we must face our problems.

We eagerly work through anxieties instead of ignoring them. Then they don't get bigger. This also helps us with our spiritual growth because we learn to do what we can to face the cause of our anxiety. Then we turn the rest over to our Higher Power. Real peace is not a lack of problems. Real peace comes from facing up to challenges.

Anxiety tells me there is a problem,
so I can face it, and learn and grow
from dealing with it.

MAY

• MAY 1 •

Conscious Contact

The task ahead of us is never as great as the Power behind us.

—*Anonymous*

Step Eleven improves our conscious contact with God. We prepare ourselves for whatever is to come when we ask only to do the will of God. The more we practice this Step, the better we get at hearing what God is telling us. Our sixth sense of intuition becomes our main sense. We begin to intuitively know what to do.

We shouldn't be surprised that we find ourselves in service. What better task is there for us than to carry the message? Step Eleven keys us into our power. Step Twelve exercises that power where it can do good. It is good to practice Step Eleven before we attempt to do anything, even get out of bed in the morning.

I focus on establishing contact with and turning my will over to my Higher Power before I attempt to do anything. Step Eleven opens my ears and my heart to what I am supposed to accomplish.

Friendship

Friendship of a kind that cannot easily be reversed tomorrow must have its roots in common interests and shared belief.
—Barbara W. Tuchman

We find the meaning of friendship in our fellowship. We no longer take hostages or allow ourselves to be hostages. We give and take freely in a spirit of good-natured affection. The friendship we find in our program is one where hidden agendas are left at the door. We relate to one another as human beings and fellow travelers. We leave sharp, jealous attitudes in our old life, where they belong.

We are careful to honor each individual. We remember that every person we meet has something to teach us. When we extend our hand to a person who is still suffering, we do not forget that it wasn't so long ago someone extended a hand to us.

I find myself able to become friends with individuals I disliked at one time. They may not have changed, but I most certainly have. The world in general has become a much friendlier place.

Changing Attitudes

The program is education without graduation.
—Anonymous

We can never escape from reality. We must adapt to the real world no matter how different and difficult it seems. We can't change the *facts* of life, but we can change our *attitudes* toward them. That's the purpose of the program, where we learn to cope without returning to the false courage and comfort of our addiction.

Stress and pressure are enemies of serenity. When they threaten to overcome us, we remember that they have been trying to make people escape into substances for ages. The healthy attitude we work for doesn't believe that stress and pressure come our way because "life isn't fair." It's important to our recovery that we remember, "We don't have attitudes; they have us."

I'm learning new attitudes toward old problems and new solutions for them, by working my program. I am learning to live in the real world.

Winning Attitude

If I should lose, let me stand by the road
and cheer as the winners go by.

—Berton Bradley

If we are to be among the winners in the recovery from addiction and obsession, we must maintain the attitude of success. Winners in any Twelve Step program take fearless inventories, correct shortcomings, and willingly make amends. By taking charge of ourselves in this manner, we neither blame nor credit others or events. With confidence and willingness, we hold *ourselves* responsible for our lives.

We take responsibility for our pre-program faults and conduct. We can then count ourselves among those who, with the help of our Higher Power, can control compulsive and excessive behavior. But we don't do it with pride. We do it with humility and gratitude.

I will begin to lose hold of a winning attitude
if I choose to leave spiritual growth to chance.
I must make life happen, not let it happen to me.

A Way of Life

The Twelve Step way of life is meant to be bread for daily living, not cake for special occasions.

—*Anonymous*

The glow of early recovery usually wears off after a little while. The pink cloud of "wow, this is the greatest thing I have ever run into" subsides after time in the program. We are called to action at some point. There is much work ahead of us in recovery. This is not the kind of work that can be crammed into a couple of weekend follow-ups. The fellowship is a way of life.

When we checked the last time, life was still lived one day at a time. Recovery is a bond we make with ourselves, before God, for the rest of our lives. We are reminded, "them which stops going to meetings are not present at meetings to hear what happens to them which stops going to meetings!"

I may have begun recovery to get the heat off my back, but I have learned the program is a way of life for the rest of my life.

• MAY 6 •

Purpose in Life

The reward of a thing well done
is to have done it.
—Ralph Waldo Emerson

The same miracle that started our recovery from addiction gave us a chance for a second life. It also brought us a purpose in life. This was something we had lacked for years. This purpose for our life makes it possible to achieve a state of happiness and peace of mind.

This purpose is to help others. Unless our hearts are filled with the principles of our new way of life, we are not doing our best. The spiritual growth that comes from pursuing a purpose in life makes each day a joy for us and makes our existence worthwhile. Long-timers remind us, "Be as enthusiastic about your recovery as you were about your addiction."

I never want to say, "This I must do." I want to say, "This I want to do." Serving a purpose in life is only a small repayment for the gift of recovery.

Prayer

Who comes from prayer a better man,
his prayer is answered.

—George Meredith

We learn that prayer is only a wish away. When we wished for recovery more than anything in the world, we found it. Thus our wishes became our prayers. It was that simple.

We discover in recovery that prayer is best when it is a conversation with a Higher Power. It isn't just a one-way speech where we tell God what we expect to have happen. It isn't a time to try to bargain with God. We listen as well as ask. Then meditation joins with prayer.

When life beats us to our knees, our only recourse is to stay on our knees and start praying.

When my prayers aren't answered right away,
that doesn't mean that God is denying them.
The answers will come in God's time, not mine.
The answers will be God's answers, not mine.

Expect a Miracle

Don't quit five minutes before
the miracle happens.
—*Anonymous*

When we came into the program, most of us had very little to show for our lives. We believed in nothing. We had experienced great disappointments. The greedy creditor that was our addiction had stripped away everything of meaning to us. We were left with nothing but pain and misery.

Now we hear incredible stories of recovery. People tell how, by following certain simple instructions and honestly working a program, they were freed from the grasp of their addiction.

Every once in a while we hear a story that sounds remarkably like our own. We are told that through work and the help of a Higher Power, we, too, can receive a miracle.

The most important miracle I can expect and count on each day is the freedom from my addiction. I can trust that if I stay close to the program, the miracle will be repeated, one day at a time.

• MAY 9 •

Trust

A person who doesn't trust themselves
can never trust others.

—Anonymous

Our fellowship provides a realistic opportunity to trust again. We learn to accept people for who they are. We do not place expectations on others. We discover our fellow travelers have had experiences similar to our own and that the issues they struggle with are issues we have in common. We learn not to wrap up all our hopes and dreams in another person. We reserve this relationship for our Higher Power.

Our recovery allows us to live in a world where people have flaws, where mistakes are made, where we might be let down and hurt. It is equally true, however, that we can find joy, companionship, and a warm fellowship if we allow ourselves to trust. We no longer demand that the world change so we can trust it.

First I learned to trust the program.
Now I've begun to trust myself
and others again.

Touching Hands

If only all the hands that reach could touch.
—Mary A. Loberg

When we were using, we may have been surrounded by people, but we felt alone. When we were beaten down to the pits of despair, we reached for helping hands. We found many extended to touch ours.

We can never stand so tall as when we stoop to reach the searching hands of those who may need our help. We know that the hands we touch will give us still more strength to work our program and carry our message of love.

Now we, too, are willing to reach out to help others who are still suffering, whether they're in the program or not. We want to give them the "hand up" we got from our friends and sponsor.

Unless my hands touch others, my recovery program will not survive. This union of hands is one of the secrets of its success.

• MAY 11 •

If Only . . .

The real fault is to have faults
and not amend them.
— Confucius

The Ninth Step allows us to close circles that have been open too long. We finally can take the "if onlies" of our lives and make the appropriate amends, including those to ourselves. Those we cannot make directly, we ask our Higher Power to make for us.

Our program has allowed us to see that we are not perfect people. We have many faults. But in the middle of this imperfection, we are also forgiven, loved, and filled with hope. We are promised that God can remove many of the character defects that have harmed us and others.

Our Tenth Step urges us not to allow "if onlies" to linger. We must take immediate steps to admit our mistakes and ask our Higher Power for help.

When I hear myself say "if only,"
the quickest way to move forward
is to repeat the Serenity Prayer.

Accepting Ourselves

Wherever you go, there you are.
—Anonymous

There was once a time when we thought the grass was greener on the other side of the road. We knew people with whom we would trade lives in a minute. We even searched out new identities in new towns and cities. We thought we were looking for life when we changed our geography. The truth was different: we were really trying to escape our lives.

Somebody once said the only problem with taking a trip is having to take ourselves. How true this was for us before we found the program. Our biggest fear in finding who we really were was that we'd discover we were no different than we appeared to be.

Our challenge in recovery has been to learn to love ourselves. We have had to be forgiven for the shabby way we've treated ourselves.

I am a person with faults to be sure, but I am basically good and getting better, one day at a time. Wherever I go, I'm happy to find that there I am.

Taking Aim

Not failure, but low aim, is crime.
—James Russell Lowell

It is more rewarding to aim at something and fail than to set our targets on nothing and score bull's-eyes. We continue to set goals for ourselves and not be upset when we fall short. On the other hand, we can never be smug when we reach a goal.

We also need to set realistic goals. If our goal is to please everyone, for instance, we will fail. No person has ever been admired, or even approved of, by all those around them.

Seeking perfect scores can only make us miserable. Doing the best we can do at any given time is all we can ask of ourselves. We may not be applauded or even accepted, and perhaps very few will notice our accomplishments. But we will know, and our Higher Power will know. And that's all that counts.

If some fail to see my accomplishments,
I don't consider them my enemies. Nor do I
assume that "if I've failed to impress them,
it must mean nobody likes me."

Self-Pity

P.L.O.M. = Poor Little Old Me.

—Anonymous

Nobody will ever grow spiritually as long as they are soaked in self-pity. Self-pity is a smokescreen we throw up to disguise anger, resentment, fear, envy, aggression, guilt, impatience, and procrastination. Self-pity is the cover-up emotion. It is an excuse for not taking action. We make no progress when we are sitting on the pity pot, because we are not recognizing the true feelings that are hidden behind the self-pity.

Self-pity is a sign of self-centeredness. There is no greater alibi for not loving and sharing, or for not being grateful or humble. A positive outlook can rid us of self-pity. We no longer demand constant attention and sympathy from everyone. We stop being martyrs.

Feelings of "poor little old me" tell me that I am afraid of failure. I must admit my limitations, set new goals, and move into positive action.

Escaping Dullness

Men are disturbed not by things but by the views they take of them.

—Epictetus

If everyone in recovery followed the principles of our Twelve Step program exactly the same way, sharing would be dull and boring. The Steps are constant, but each of us in recovery work them differently, to whatever degree gives us the most serenity and spiritual growth.

If all of us lived the guiding principles of recovery by habit, mechanically, without thinking, the routine would become uninteresting and tiring. We must not be afraid of adding new ideas that work for us to the tried-and-true manner of thinking we find in our fellowship. Using our imagination properly will keep recovery continuously fresh and rewarding.

Even far-out ideas can be useful to me if they inspire thinking and prevent complacency.

Being Practical

Theories are like the tail feathers of a rooster, highly ornamental but not much use in a high wind.

—Arthur E. Holt

Theories for effective living are important, but unless we put them into action, they are worthless. The Twelve Steps and the slogans are among the theories that have been tested by millions who have put them into action. They have withstood the "high winds" of living.

Meditation on some theories may do nothing for our recovery except make us feel better. Even this is useful.

By working the kinds of behavior and thinking in our lives that we find in theories, we make those theories into practical realities.

It is less important to look well than to be well. Theories by themselves look good. Working them makes us good.

What I ask for while I am on my knees in prayer is never as vital to me as what I do with the answers I receive once I am back on my feet.

Intellectualizing

Don't intellectualize, utilize.
—Anonymous

Many times we waste our minds by using them too much. A mind out of control can waste a life. Our mind can tell us we are better or less than another. It can tell us we need things we don't, and that we should fear situations we needn't. The power of the mind to intellectualize a life into a mess is amazing.

Our program should be utilized not intellectualized. We do not need to waste time debating points about the program. We will not resolve with other intellectuals whether or not alcoholism and drug addiction are physical diseases or bad habits. The point, for us addicts, is that we will waste our life, die, or go insane if we do not stay in recovery. All we have to do is look around a meeting room to see whether or not it works.

The Steps tell me HOW the program works. The Traditions tell me WHY it works. My sponsor and fellow members show me THAT it works.

If It Works

If it works, don't fix it.
—Anonymous

We all like to tailor our lives to suit ourselves. But we have found that the more we stamp the impression of our ego on people, the more we push them away. The more we try to control situations, the more out of control they become.

When we started our program, we needed to read "only the black" in our Big Book. We don't need to try to improve the fellowship by reading between the lines. If we just pay attention to what the old-timers tell us, we will save ourselves much misery. We don't need to modify the program to fit our needs. We need to fit our needs into the program.

We are so used to problems that sometimes, even if something works, we make it a problem because we're used to it. We have made ourselves experts at handling crises because we don't know how to handle success. We are strangers to things that work.

To let working things work seems strange and unfamiliar. If it's working, please don't let me fix it.

Healthy Thinking

Knowledge of "the answers" never made anyone relapse. It was failing to practice "the answers" known.

—*Anonymous*

The quality of our lives will always depend on the way we think. When anxiety, stress, and tension begin to threaten our hard-won peace of mind, we must not blame our retreat from serenity on outside forces. We can get back in line with comfortable living when we remind ourselves that we have been thinking wrong about something.

It may be complacency: "I've got all the right answers." Perhaps we've been thinking selfishly or suffering twinges of jealousy and envy. Are we viewing others with anger or resentment, being fearful of falling short of goals? We learn in recovery to examine our thinking.

Positive thinking is my guarantee that serenity will continue to make me willing to accept myself as the author of my own attitudes, not a victim of outside forces.

Shortcomings

Search out shortcomings and correct them.
—Anonymous

One of the hardest things to do is to look at our own shortcomings when we are angry at someone. It seems impossible to believe at such times that something may be wrong with us. This is the reason we are so often instructed to count to ten. When we find ourselves so out of sorts, so internally disrupted, there is usually something wrong with us.

It is our first obligation to take care of ourselves. It is out of love for ourselves that we withdraw and take a spot-check inventory. The spot-check inventory does not demean or humiliate us. On the contrary, the purpose is to speak with God briefly, check our vital signs, and clean out our connections.

I always need my connection with God.
Nothing works without a clear, clean,
strong, conscious contact with
my Higher Power.

Jealousy

The jealous are troublesome to others,
but a torment to themselves.

—William Penn

The disappearance of jealousy is a wonder to behold in the life of a recovering person. The world before our program was a world of want for us. We never seemed to have enough of anything. Nothing was ever quite right. There was a constant sense of an incomplete world and that life wasn't fair.

What was so painful for us was our wicked jealousy of those who seemed to have what we wanted. This created deep resentments.

Now life is different for us. We have more than we can ever use because the supply is limitless. What we desire now can't be measured. It's there for the taking. And it has nothing to do with what we wanted before. Our spiritual awakening has revealed a world of abundance and fulfillment.

The program has given me what I need.
I am no longer jealous of what others have.

Seeking Privacy

Let there be space in your togetherness.
—Kahlil Gibran

Identifying with those who help our recovery by sharing experiences, strengths and hopes is one reason why our program works. As we relate more closely to fellow members and our affection for them grows, we must be aware that danger lies in the belief that we all live alike.

We cannot try to possess others or work their program for them. Each is an individual, following the same principles in his or her way to the best of their ability and within limitations. We must always give others the privacy their recovery requires.

We remember that we are responsible for ourselves alone. Our recovery, our well-being, our happiness are all ultimately our own responsibility.

Privacy is a precious gift to all who need
ample time to pray, meditate, and plan each day.
Yet, in being alone with shared problems,
I am never truly alone.

Trusting Others

The three Ts of gratitude to repay the program for our recovery: our TIME, our TALENT, our TRUST.

—*Anonymous*

In our recovery, we are building trust in others and in ourselves. For the first time in our lives, we know that we can reveal ourselves completely to others without fear of being put down. When we get stuck with negative thoughts, it is important to find the strength of sharing with others in the program.

At the same time, we are aware that others are placing trust in us not to use their sharing to benefit ourselves or to belittle them. By exchanging confidences and personal experiences, we are truly expressing our ability to love.

We hear that our entire program rests on the principle of mutual trust. We trust God, we trust the Twelve Steps, and we trust each other. The Second Tradition states that our leaders are but "trusted servants."

When I share with others, I am also aware that they need me, just as I need them.

Listening

Before engaging your mouth,
put your mind in gear.
—*Anonymous*

Our world is full of speechmakers who would serve better if they learned the importance of listening. The ability to *hear* is stressed within our group. It is true that we owe it to fellow members to tell the valuable lessons we learn while dealing with reality. But by listening, we can find truth from outside ourselves, too. Old-timers remind us to "take the cotton out of our ears and put it in our mouth."

An old proverb says, "When the pupil is ready, the teacher will appear." Another tells us, "Find a teacher and you find a friend." When we learn to be attentive, we continue to be students long after our school years are over. Even when we read, we can listen well to truths.

One gift of being a good listener is to hear unexpectedly some truth I may have been told but was not ready to hear.

Reality

The Twelve Steps can only take us
as far as we allow them to take us.
—*Anonymous*

We grew up believing that we could avoid the pain of life by retreating into a dream world. A short time of sharing in a Twelve Step group, however, will prove that fantasy is more dangerous than fact simply because it lacks substance. We cannot afford guesswork; any decision must be based on truths.

We find that reality never changes, but our attitude toward it can. We are not responsible for what happens to us, but our reactions to experiences are ours alone. Reality tells us not to waste time avoiding being what we dislike being, but to bear down on becoming the person we want to be. Reality gives us simple, concrete answers rather than empty dreams.

How I react to reality makes my reality. If I
react to anger with love instead of more anger,
or if I react to a crisis with faith instead of fear,
I am creating a reality of love and faith
instead of anger and fear.

Character

Fame is what you have taken. Character is what you give. When to this truth you waken, then you begin to live.

—Bayard Taylor

Long-timers continually tell newcomers to strive to build a strong character for use in facing the world's realities. Sometimes they leave the impression that character is what others think about us. But the opinion others have about us is not important. Character is what we are, not what others think we are.

We are not born with character. It is developed through patience and much humility. It is what we are *in the dark*. Our character is revealed by an outer show of an inner glow. It is our reserve force for living. It is more useful than talent and shows itself best during our contact with others.

Today I'll remember my character can be a force that respects truth, develops will and spirit, accents positive action, and makes all of these assets evident to other people.

Success

Success is a ladder that cannot be climbed with your hands in your pockets.

—American saying

All too often, we hear someone's success explained as "a stroke of good luck." Success and progress are no more the result of good luck than failure is the result of bad luck. Natural ability is of little use unless we develop habits of hard work. Brilliance is born in some, but labor or action is of greater importance.

We perform to the best of our ability when we work for the work's sake, not for any hope of fame. Success results from hard work and confidence in our judgment. The degree of success depends on the amount of good judgment used. Good advice and judgment from others is helpful, but the doing is entirely ours.

Success is simply the use of the abilities I have. I must treat them as practical tools, not magical gifts. Nobody travels my road for me.

Honesty

I hope I shall follow firmness of virtue enough to maintain that I consider the most enviable of all titles—the character of an honest man.

—George Washington

Happiness in recovery and in society depends on our honesty. We create pain for others, *and* ourselves, when we are dishonest. True honesty begins within each of us and flows out to touch those around us. If we are to be true to society, and to ourselves, we cannot feel one thing in our hearts and outwardly speak different views.

There is no such thing as too much honesty. When we practice honesty in all our affairs, we discover that the reason for being honest is not because it is expected of us, but because we find that honesty avoids problems and makes our life happier.

When I am honest with myself and others, I am making progress toward greatness of character.

Being Alone

ON THE BEAM: Getting on with the business of living by using the program.

—*Anonymous*

Most of the joys of living come during times of sharing with others. But we would miss a lot if we didn't make time in which to be entirely alone with our thoughts and take inventory of ourselves.

Preparing for the next day by examining the one we've just finished gives us a head start on tomorrow. Both activities are done when we are alone.

Alone and silent in thought, we need to examine how well we have used the day. Only then are we able to tackle the first hours of a new day.

By examining my day as it ends, I can weigh the wins and the losses to strengthen my chances of success with my plans for tomorrow. Then I turn it all over to my Higher Power.

Easy Does It

It isn't the load that weighs us down,
it's the way we carry it.

—*Anonymous*

There is a saying in the entertainment world that it takes most performers at least twenty years to become overnight successes. Many a person who is impatient to set the world on fire could be served best by a discussion on "Easy does it" and "One Step at a time." Like Rome, character wasn't built in a day.

When we try to climb ladders several steps at a time, we invite accidents. But the advice "slow but sure" doesn't mean not making the effort. Progress is always more lasting when made with caution. We solve problems as they arise, rather than trying to move around them.

I risk losing serenity if I let impatience
force me into trying to do too much
in too short a time.

Backing Off

The more I turn outward to others the stronger I become within. Mistakes are facts of life. It is my response to them that counts.

—*Anonymous*

It's brave to believe that nothing is impossible, but such an attitude isn't real. It's impossible to change things we have said and actions we wish we hadn't taken.

We can learn from older and wiser members that we can be happy without winning every battle. The most important battle we must win is to stay clean and sober.

We may have some rude awakenings if we think we have to fight any other battle than staying abstinent. It's foolhardy not to back away from the impossible just so we can feel heroic.

Each time we back off from confusion, we buy valuable time to find a better way. There is no disgrace in changing directions when the way we're going is wrong.

When I back off from things I can't change, I win.

Turn It Over

Freedom is not something that anybody can be given; freedom is something people take and people are as free as they want to be.

—*James Baldwin*

Problems seem to be made of a thousand little "Its": our family, our weight, our self-image, our job, our career, our relationships. These little Its become big Its as we magnify them. Our Its soon become dragons that devour us and chase us from place to place. The Its in our lives are always people, places, and things we cannot control. They are always outside us and we let them attack us as enemies.

The fellowship helps us see that usually Its are manifestations of us. Therefore, when Its bother us, it is just us bothering ourselves. When our Its strike out at us, it is us beating up on ourselves. When the program tells us to turn Its over, it quietly suggests that we give it to God. The fight has always been from within. That battle of is one we always lose.

I always find a safe harbor when I turn it (my will, my problems, and my life) over to the care of my Higher Power.

Procrastination

Procrastination is the thief of time.
—Edward Young

The habit of putting off actions until things get better is one of the most destructive detours from common sense we can make. Delays never make problems go away; they only make success harder to attain. If we shy away from bringing out problems to others, we are sure to cause stress and misunderstanding.

Quite often, postponing facing up to reality results from fear that others will laugh at us. That is self-pity in action. Solutions come from direct and specific action. We always remember that others in our group give us "the right to be wrong," knowing that a change in direction is always possible for anyone with problems. Procrastination wastes precious time.

When I procrastinate about solving problems,
I am only making sure they will get worse.
Let me remember that solutions come
from taking action.

Expectations

Stop expecting too much from yourself.
—*Anonymous*

When there is too wide a gap between standards we set for ourselves and our actual achievement, unhappiness follows. If we can't improve the performance, we should lower the demands. When we are true to ourselves, we come to expect only that which we are capable of doing. As we grow each day in recovery, we are able to do more.

What we expect from ourselves can change the next day. It is very important that through our meetings and conversations with fellow members, we keep close tabs on our development. We find out that life is for living, and it is better lived when we do our assignments every day.

We are really never given more than we can do. As long as we have realistic goals, we will be given what we need to succeed.

Today I'll remember that when my expectations are too high, I get stuck and down on myself.

The Value of Time

> *Remember, the pursuit of happiness is futile. Happiness, peace of mind, and serenity are the results of the way YOU think God would have you live.*
>
> —*Anonymous*

Relaxation and recreation are important to us all. Rest and entertainment prepare us for the challenges of life by giving us new energy and purpose.

During our sharing, we can all learn to use time well by preparing for the future. Of course, living in the *now* as well as we can, one day at a time, is our main concern.

A story goes that a carpenter was asked why he was repairing a judge's bench chair with extra care, and he replied, "Because I want it comfortable when I sit in it myself." And he actually did earn that honor some years later! Setting realistic goals now is using time well by preparing for the future.

If I didn't plan for the needs of my future,
it would be like not planting seeds
to build tomorrow's forests.

• JUNE 5 •

Forgiveness

Never does the human soul appear so strong as when it foregoes revenge and dares forgive an injury.

—E.H. Chapin

Unless we can freely forgive others, we will never be able to forgive ourselves. The freedom to give ourselves a second (or third or fourth) chance to right a wrong or perform a helpful act opens the way to spiritual growth.

Unqualified forgiveness, both for others and for ourselves, keeps us from being overcome by guilt or shame over not being kind to ourselves and those around us. Forgiveness is a first step in making emotional progress; all succeeding steps become easier.

My sponsor told me to imagine climbing a beautiful hill and sitting in the sunlight, then to imagine my enemy climbing the same hill and sitting with me. Then I was to leave my enemy in the sunlight while I walked down the hill. This, my sponsor said, was forgiveness.

The First Hour

Every recovery from addiction begins with one clean and sober hour.

—Anonymous

It is amazing to watch a television program and see how the most complicated life situations are resolved in less than thirty minutes. Those of us who have made a heavy diet of television probably wonder deep down why our problems are not solved quickly in recovery. When we were drinking and drugging, thirty minutes was plenty of time to dissolve a problem into oblivion.

Recovery isn't like TV. We can't change the channel if we don't like the program.

There are two facts we can't escape in our program and recovery: treatment begins with one clean and sober hour, and the cure will take a lifetime.

The good news is that the focus of recovery is on the treatment, not the cure. And while there might not always be something good on TV, there's always something good on the program.

I will remember that recovery is a process, not an event.

• JUNE 7 •

Came to Believe

Find something bigger than yourself in which to believe. Believe in God or be God!

—*Anonymous*

Self-centered, egotistic, materialistic people score lowest of all in measuring happiness. We all think it is easy to see that money doesn't buy happiness. Yet everyone seems to give their all to obtaining money. We all know that we will never find the meaning of our lives in another person. Yet how much time have we spent looking for such a person?

All our striving for the *things* of this world has given us little or no happiness. We always end up with either nothing to believe in or believing in the wrong things.

Whenever we make a god out of ourselves, someone else, or our material possessions, we bring misery down around us.

There is something bigger than myself that I must believe in and trust completely for my peace and happiness. That is my Higher Power.

Willingness

H.O.W. = Honesty, Open-mindedness, Willingness.

—*Anonymous*

H.O.W. is a pattern for character and spiritual growth. We must approach all challenges with Honest intentions and Open-minded tolerance. But only Willingness will start us toward goals. When the willingness is great, the difficulties cannot be great. If we are willing to accept and to act with dedication, nothing can stop us as long as our goals are for spiritual rewards.

Willingness can simply mean that we are ready and well-prepared to face challenges. But we must be cautious not to mistake *willful* for *willing*. The first insists that things happen our way and on our terms. But willingness rids us of fears and prepares us to choose wisely.

The program tells me that "willingness is the key" and "willingness without action is fantasy." These are essentials of recovery.

Secrets

We are only as sick as our secrets.
—Anonymous

The shadowy world of our addiction kept us always in search of new places to hide. Each time we told a lie, we had to develop an elaborate cover for the lie. Every time we broke a promise, cheated on our loved ones, stole from our job, we would make up new stories to cover our tracks. When we got caught in a lie, we would create even more complicated lies to cover up the truth. When anyone threatened our addiction, we would go further underground to make sure its needs were met.

Our recovery has allowed us an opportunity to be shown the way out of the maze of lies and secrets. They cannot co-exist with an honest life. If we are to be entirely honest in all our affairs, the cat must come out of the bag. The truth will set us free.

I'm not going to be sick anymore. There can be no lies or secrets in my life of recovery. I must always be ready to be entirely honest.

• JUNE 10 •

People-Pleasing

Formula for failure: trying to please everyone.

—*Anonymous*

It has done us no good to set standards we could not reach. On many occasions, we adopted goals that couldn't be reached from the beginning. We allowed our identities to become tied in with pleasing people. If we suffered rejection, we collapsed into a quivering heap. Each time we wrapped ourselves up in a package for someone to pass judgment on, we set ourselves up for failure.

We know we are not God. We must realize no other human being is God, either. We can't ask any person to judge us. We can't judge anyone else. The foundation of our program is the decision we made in Step Three to turn our will and life over to the care of God. This is the formula for success. Try pleasing God, not other people.

I can't build my life and recovery on always trying to please others. My road to success is pleasing my Higher Power.

Choices

Before I came to the program, I had no choice. I had to use: now I have a choice.

—*Anonymous*

One of the freedoms we enjoy is that of making choices. Only through experience and the wise advice of others can we determine if our choices are right. Even if some are risky, we cannot settle for being wishy-washy. Straddling issues achieves nothing. Bad choices can be corrected by second chances. There is no shame in delaying a choice while we examine all possibilities.

C.H.O.I.C.E. is Courage, Humility, Optimism, Industry, Caution, and Energy. When we choose recovery, we use all of these things. And the end result is H.A.P.P.I.N.E.S.S.: Humility, Awakening, Plenty, Program, Insight, New life, Excitement, Spirituality, and Serenity.

There is no "right" choice, only choices made after asking my Higher Power for direction and listening carefully for the answer. If I do that correctly and the choice still seems "wrong," then I haven't understood God's will for me.

Frustration

Nothing is unthinkable, nothing impossible to the balanced person, provided it arises out of the needs of life and is dedicated to life's further developments.

—Lewis Mumford

In recovery we walk one foot in front of the other. We live life "One day at a time." We "Live and let live." These slogans we have in the program help with the frustrations we experience in everyday living. The fact of the matter is, most of us have spent so many years forcing our will on each situation that it is difficult to stop.

It takes practice and patience to slow down and let life come to us, rather than rushing off to make things happen. Our Higher Power has a sense of time and timing that will be revealed to us slowly. Frustration will not move a clock forward, change a traffic light from red to green, or make us younger. Frustration will only block our serenity.

The Steps teach me that it is sometimes necessary to do absolutely nothing. I can hear better when I am quiet.

Tomorrow

The future you shall know when it has come; before then, forget it.

—Aeschylus

The fellowship keeps us grounded in the current moment. We learn to live today. Our planning and scheming and dreaming about tomorrow becomes less time consuming. The idea of living one day at a time makes sense to us. Our program teaches us that life is not about to happen, it is happening, and each moment is important.

When we concentrated only on the future, we couldn't be happy with today. We thought if we could only get to tomorrow, things would be better. Tomorrow never comes, so we were always trapped in a hopeless situation. Now we live one day at a time and grow moment by moment.

Recovery is about today and living life in the present. Since I no longer have to manage the universe, I have only myself to worry about today. I can let my Higher Power take care of tomorrow.

Truth

Great is truth. Fire cannot burn it nor water drown it.
—Alexandre Dumas

The importance of truth is stressed often during our Twelve Step discussions. Truth is the foundation of all knowledge. It is the standard by which all our actions are judged. Truth can never be bought. There is no happy medium in truth. All things must be either true or false.

Unless an activity begins with truth, it will be impossible to progress successfully. The advice "truth or silence" warns us of the possible harm from hurriedly made statements. Love and kindness must accompany truth even if we, as the giver or receiver, are pained by the truth. Our program teaches us that truth can do no more than present things as they really exist.

For me to work my program successfully, I must always work from a foundation of truth.

Accepting Ourselves

Humility is our acceptance of ourselves.
—Anonymous

It is strange how we can go to school and learn a lot of facts, but never learn much along the way about ourselves. We can take up nursing, teaching, counseling, giving ourselves to the needs of others, while never having our own needs met.

Why does it seem as if it is easier to solve the problems of the world than to solve our own problems? We simply don't know ourselves very well. When we look into a mirror and attempt to understand ourselves, our conclusions about what we see are usually very different from what a friend sees. When we finally take the time and make ourselves a priority, we make a startling discovery. There exists within us at all times a Higher Power that is the builder of all successes and our comforter during times of trial.

I understand myself only in relation to my Higher Power. The image I see and the identity I have is then one of humility before that Power. Humility is my acceptance of myself.

Good People

I sought my soul, but my soul I could not see; I sought my God, but my God eluded me; I sought my brother, and I found all three.

— William Blake

The fellowship is filled with good people. We meet men and women who have suffered greatly as a result of their addiction. Sometimes we have to talk with them to find the goodness underneath their many layers of scars. Before finding the program, these men and women, like us, had never been able to find what they were looking for in life.

We were looking for love in all the wrong places. It was truly painful to be out of touch with our soul and to have no conscious contact with our Higher Power. This was the source of most of our pain. We know this because it is now the source of all our peace, joy, and serenity.

I can remember the moment I found
my soul and my Higher Power.
After all the searching outside myself,
I found them deep within me.

Confidence

I want, by understanding myself, to understand others. I want to be all that I am capable of being.
—Katherine Mansfield

We cannot make our life worth living until we have faith in our freedom of choice. This is the basis of confidence, the one asset that guarantees us success in what we have come to believe. Our program warns us that we cannot achieve if we fear our ability to learn and to grow. Our primary confidence is in ourselves. This is a great step away from the feeling of failure we had in the depths of addiction.

We build self-confidence by working toward who we want to be. Each Step takes us closer to that person. The closer we get, the more confidence we have that the program works for us.

My self-confidence is growing because I want to be all I can be.

• JUNE 18 •

Emotional Stress

No man is an island, entire of itself . . . each is a piece of the continent, a part of the main.

—*John Donne*

When we find ourselves in the grip of emotional stress, we force ourselves to be outgoing, rather than retreating into isolation. The mind is a terrible place in which to live. Daydreams are fine, but they all too quickly turn into nightmares. Our minds magnify our emotions. Our minds tell us that we are more in love than we are, angrier than we are, happier than we are, and mostly more miserable than we are. When we retreat into isolation, we become prey to stinking thinking.

There is no peace of mind when the mind is allowed to work its own way. We need people. We need the fellowship. When people are hard to find, we use the phone. The best medicine we have for emotional stress is to become involved in service.

Stress can cause me to hide inside myself, thinking no one else understands. I need to reach out instead, and share my feelings with others who can help.

Unselfishness

Modesty and unselfishness—these are the virtues which men praise.

—André Maurois

We continually work toward unselfishness. To be unselfish is to be useful. When we are selfish, we are useless to others and to ourselves. By hoarding everything for ourselves, not only material things but even good healthy thoughts and feelings, we are depriving not only others but ourselves. Material things are cold and can't return our love. Good thoughts and feelings will soon shrivel and die unless we pass them on to others.

The Twelfth Step tells us we must give away what we have to keep what we have gained. So we learn that it is impossible to give without receiving and equally impossible to receive without giving back. Always, giving brings rewards such as satisfaction and self-worth. This is passing it on.

I know that sharing increases good things, while selfishness decreases them.

Fear

Fear is the darkroom where
negatives are developed.
—Michael Pritchard

Fear haunts so many of us. Fear is behind all our resentments. It attacks us when we are alone and isolated. It can wreak havoc on us when we are by ourselves. We see only dark clouds over our heads; all appears hopeless and negative.

We have meetings because we do not face our fears alone. The program is not a program of us talking to ourselves. We need the fellowship and our fellow travelers.

When we overcome the fear of asking for help, the program will give us all the support we need. But the fellowship is not composed of mind readers. We have to open our mouths and share our struggles. Remember, when we share experience, we can also be sharing our troubles. We share problems as well as solutions.

My fears have a way of dissolving
when I share them with my sponsor
and fellow members.

The Recovering Young

The program is a school in which we are all learners and all teachers regardless of age.

—*Anonymous*

The younger generation in the program embraces the program with enthusiasm that can only be attributed to the young. And, of course, abstinence is never wasted on anyone, let alone young people whose whole lives are in front of them.

Today a larger percentage of young men and women are flooding recovery units and meeting halls. Although older members may have long abstinence, they are often bested by the eagerness the young devote to working their program.

Many who are new to recovery ask the same question: "What will I do with all my time now that I've stopped using?" Young people learn that service work and sober activities with fellow members keep them busy.

I know the future of our program is secure because of the many good young people who are working it.

The Older Member

Older people are always young enough to learn, with profit.
—Aeschylus

An older member who has a desire to live in moderation in all things has as much need for recovery as a young person who surrenders and accepts their problem. When someone has the spiritual experience that gives them a chance for a second life, they know it's never too late to begin to change lifetime habits.

Many an older member has decided that they not only can save their lives, but that they can make those lives worth saving. They are determined to shake the bondage that addiction has created. With determination they plan to add years to their lives and life to their years.

There is no generation gap in recovery from addiction. One of the miracles is that both young and old can find a mutual caring and understanding once they surrender to a common reality.

Early Recovery

Spirituality is the ability to
get our minds off ourselves.
—*Anonymous*

The early days of recovery were a strange time for us. We were used to a very different lifestyle. There were so many new things coming into our lives all at once. Everything was whirling. We stuck close to our sponsor and home group. We needed a touchstone to make sense out of what was happening.

The early days of recovery were times of physical healing. We knew we were sick. Some of us didn't realize how sick we were. We went slow and kept our eyes, our minds, and our hearts focused on our First Step.

We didn't find instant spirituality in those days. That was okay. There would be time enough for that; first, we had to get started. After time on the program, after we had worked some Steps, we were asked to get our minds off ourselves. This was the time when we started making progress with our spiritual lives.

I have learned that spirituality is the
ability to get my mind off myself.

Effort

We are responsible for the effort,
not the outcome.

—*Anonymous*

During our addictive years, it was a common practice to work things backward. We were known to eat our dessert before our main meal, to celebrate before we won, to assume the outcome before the event.

The problem with this behavior is that it takes no account of reality. Things move from beginning to end. The alphabet reads from A to Z. This seems so simple, but it can be tricky for people who are used to taking shortcuts. Our program is best utilized by starting with Step One and moving through each Step in sequence. We often hear of people Two-Stepping the program, moving from Step One immediately to Step Twelve. This practice often causes relapse.

It is essential that I put all my effort into every Step. If I do, the outcome will take care of itself. All I affect is my effort, and that will always speak for itself.

Count Your Blessings

Gratitude is the attitude.
—Anonymous

There are many adjustments to be made in our recovery. We must be careful how we judge our progress. The program provides us with a new pair of glasses to see our new world. Those glasses were uncomfortable to us at first. We saw things so differently that we sometimes questioned what we saw.

We soon discovered getting better is not about having a better car, nicer home, smarter children, better relationships, or any goal we might ever have had. Getting better is about maintaining our daily conscious contact with our Higher Power, which helps us to accept the many things in our lives.

Our world is not changing, but we know we are. When we take our daily inventory we do not count the things we have accumulated or will accumulate. We count the times we have been on the beam or off the beam. Our inventory should always end with gratitude to our Higher Power and the fellowship for one more day of freedom from our disease.

I've learned in recovery to count my blessings and work for an attitude of gratitude.

Praying

Trying to pray is praying.
—Anonymous

"Oh, God, help me! If you get me out of this mess, I'll never screw up again." This was our favorite prayer before we entered the program. We were always bargaining with God.

We have learned new prayers and a new way to talk and listen to our Higher Power. We are seeking God's will for us. Many of us had to learn how to pray. We began with very simple prayers: "God, help me know Your will for me." "Thank you, God, for helping me today."

We learn that prayer helps us with our faulty dependence on people, places, and things by giving us the insight and strength to rearrange our priorities. Prayer doesn't change God, but it changes those who pray.

Today in my prayers, I will seek my Higher Power's will for me. I no longer bargain with God.

Not God

First of all, we had to quit playing God.
It didn't work.

— *Big Book of Alcoholics Anonymous*

The game we always lose is the game of playing God. When we attempt to take absolute control over either our own lives or the life of another, we only harm ourselves or them. When we inflict our own will on a situation, all we reveal is our own fear and insecurity.

Step Two reminds us that most of our problems have been of our own making. Until we quit trying to control everyone and everything, we could find no peace. As we work the program with the belief that we're not God, today and tomorrow are far less frightening.

Many of us have been helped with the problem of grandiose thinking by the familiar slogan, "I can't, God can, I think I'll let Him."

Today I'll remember that if I try
to play God, I'm crazy.

Sharing

Not what we give but what we share.
For a gift without the giver is bare.
—J.R. Lowell

The magic of abstinence is always based on the joy of sharing. None of us can be only a giver or a receiver. In order to share, we must be both a giver and a receiver.

Nothing ever comes to someone who only holds open his arms and says, "Give to me. I'm ready to enjoy rewards." Because the rewards we receive come from the joy of giving, we must give to receive. This is called sharing.

The miracle of sharing is building the confidence that we are able to give to others and take the rewards into our hearts. Sharing brings joy to everyone involved. It is a two-way process between giving and receiving. One can't exist without the other. Recovery can't exist without either of them.

Today I'll remember that by sharing
I give to and receive from others
and they do the same for me.

• JUNE 29 •

Finding God

If God seems far away, who moved?
—Anonymous

We traveled near and far to find a relationship with God. We spent hours looking for God in nature or the stars. We listened to many enlightened speakers to obtain a glimpse of God's presence. The harder we tried to find God, the further removed God was from our lives. We lived our lives as if we had lost God. We thought that if we searched hard enough, we could find Him.

The new world we have found in recovery shows us what has always been there. While we were searching, we were never living with what we had. God will never be nearer to us than He is right now. Our responsibility in life is to keep our conscious contact with our Higher Power free and open. When God seems far away, that contact needs to be renewed.

When I meditate, pray, and keep my inventory current, God always is with me because I am with God. I no longer need to search for something that can't be lost.

Intuition

When we listen, God speaks.
When we obey, God works.
—*Anonymous*

Recovery opens up our sixth sense of intuition. This sense is our path to truth, to spirituality, to our Higher Power. The old-timers we look to for guidance always have keen intuition. They know things about us before we do. They say things to us that cut through to our core. These men and women are really no different from us, except that they have learned to trust their intuition and, therefore, their contact with their Higher Power.

We were all skeptical about the power of intuition when we were new to the fellowship. We protested that we had education, we wanted scientific proof, absolute evidence that the program worked. The old-timers who listened to our protests just shrugged their shoulders and gave us a knowing smile.

I must trust my intuition as my mind and heart are healed. I receive the promises of the program when I can respond to my intuition and base my actions on its truth.

JULY

Live with Moderation

O grant me, Heaven, a middle state
Neither too humble nor too great,
More than enough for nature's ends,
With something left to treat my friends.

— *David Mallet*

One of the biggest defects of character, a shortcoming suffered by us all, is our inability to be moderate in living. During our active addiction we did everything to extremes. We thought anything worthwhile must always be done to excess. "Too much ain't enough" was the keynote of our living. We wanted to do everything as often and as much as possible. It was all or nothing for us.

Now we try to change our behavior and thinking so there can never be too much or too little. We work for a happy middle ground. In our program we learn early that extremes in anything will accomplish nothing.

I must discard my old ideas about
living to extremes. It is now the
middle ground I seek.

Let Go and Let God

We can't carry the person, we can only carry the message. The results are in God's hands.

—Anonymous

"Let go, let God" doesn't mean we stop caring; it means we can't do it all for someone else. We in the program care deeply. We can sometimes pick up another person's pain more quickly than our own. There is a very natural inclination to want to stop the hurting. There are even times we have neglected our own well-being to help another.

We need to remember our own experience. It was not until we did our First Step that we became available for recovery. The First Step was an admission and acceptance of our powerlessness. No one did our First Step for us. This fact is true for others as well. We can't carry anyone through the Steps and expect them to understand recovery.

If my hand is holding on to someone else's too tightly, that person's hand can't hold on to God's.

Death

We surrender to win, we die to live, we suffer to get well, we give it away to keep it.

—*Anonymous*

The program teaches us not to fear death as we learn not to fear life. Death must happen for life to be born. Our addiction told us to hold on to all sorts of dead or dying realities. Our addiction prevented us from growing up. We tried to hold on to our youth rather than letting it pass away naturally.

When God called a loved one on, we fought and cursed God for not getting our permission first. When a relationship came and went we sometimes spent years mourning the loss. As death became more fearful to us, we closed ourselves off from the new life that was waiting. Our program teaches us to let go of the dead and dying, and embrace the new. We rejoice in the celebration of life.

I have come to a new reality regarding life and death because I have faced the reality of the death of my addiction and the new life of my recovery.

• JULY 4 •

Easy Does It

The great mind knows the power of gentleness.
— Robert Browning

We have learned to become gentle with ourselves and other people. The slogan "Easy does it" works in all situations. We created confusion in our lives when we lost our light touch and our soft-spoken word. We were like a tornado, upsetting everything in our path. Nothing was ever changed by our power-driven tantrums.

When we are stopped dead on the freeway, will shaking our fist at every passing car get us where we're going any faster? "Easy does it" is our way of reminding ourselves to go slow, let God work His will, everything is okay. We have learned to walk more softly and with more consideration.

I am not lazy when I slow down and take life on life's terms. I am simply tuned into the secret of how life actually works.

Humor

Pain is deeper than all thought;
laughter is higher than all pain.
—Elbert Hubbard

The world of recovery has given us back a sense of humor. We have learned to laugh at ourselves and laugh hard. The gloomy seriousness that hung over us like a dark cloud is removed and replaced. We begin to see our past history that caused us such misery in a different light. We come to appreciate the humor in our game-playing, our inflated egos, our power-driven ambitions, our grandiose plans, our perfectionism, and our silly pouting.

We've discovered laughter and humor as a medicine to heal wounds. We laugh uproariously at the stories of others as they remember their past. We don't laugh to belittle our friends, but to share in the release of our pain and the fact that times are oh, so different now.

I have gotten off my pedestal and off my pity pot and have joined the human race as just a fellow traveler. Life looks a lot funnier when both my feet are on the ground.

Employment

A man's work is rather the needful supplement to himself than the outcome of it.

—Max Beerbohm

Our time in recovery allows us to redefine our vocation. We no longer seek the "right job" to fulfill our lives. We realize the right job will not make us whole people. We are already complete and need only maintain a conscious contact with our Higher Power to remain so. We need to work and earn money so we can feed, clothe, and shelter ourselves and our loved ones, but to demand from our job any greater significance will tempt us to create a Higher Power out of our work. We know the resentment and anxiety we cause ourselves whenever we do this.

Many times in recovery we may find ourselves in positions and jobs that seem strange to us. Not to worry; God has a plan for us that we sometimes cannot understand. We remember to increase our program service work when we get too upset about our employment concerns.

The life of recovery is a vocation in itself. I will remember a job is a job. Recovery is a way of life.

Knowledge

When you know a thing, to hold that you know it, and when you do not know a thing, to allow that you do not know it: this is knowledge.

— *Confucius*

How is it we can hear so much better after we have worked our Steps? Does someone clean the wax out of our ears at night? We find ourselves able to listen to what people are actually saying, not just to what we think they are saying. Our program teaches us not to judge words before or after they are spoken. We leave judging to God. We try to learn from everybody, for each person we meet has knowledge.

Knowledge has become available to us as never before. We no longer fear new ideas and opinions that are not our own. Our recovery becomes deeper each moment we open our minds to new ideas.

Knowledge is freely offered. In turn, I keep myself growing and accepting the knowledge that comes my way. When I don't know something, I admit it. Knowing that I don't know is also knowledge.

Dreaming

Dreaming permits each and every one of us to be quietly and safely insane every night of our lives.

— *William Dement*

The mind is wildly active during sleep. We have found in recovery that it takes a long time for our minds to heal. We often wake up in the morning and wonder where we have spent the night.

We must remember that before we came into the program we did not let ourselves rest. There is a lot of processing our minds must do to catch up on all the time we numbed it closed. We may dream of returning to our active addiction. We may relive scenes so real we will swear they happened.

Not to worry. This too shall pass. We remember to keep our telephone numbers near. A late-night call to a sponsor is a great way to slay the dragons of our "drunk dreams." The key to recovery is in letting go and letting God.

As I ask God to take my dreams of the past
and replace them with the gifts of today,
my reliving of history will go away.

The Problem

Coming together is a beginning; keeping together is progress; working together is success.

—Henry Ford

One of the biggest problems of addiction began with the initial desire to increase and continue to use an addictive substance. All of us who have gotten to the point of overdoing the consumption of a substance were basically, in some manner, filling a need to be what we thought was "normal," like other people.

We were convinced we were unworthy, inadequate, afraid, and lonely whenever we compared ourselves to others. We disconnected and isolated ourselves, not only from our peers, but from our own real selves. We lived in a world of fantasy.

Our problem was more than a physical hunger for the things that made us dependent. It was also not dealing with crazy thinking, self-defeating behavior, and screwed-up emotions.

Today I'll remember addiction is two-fold: one was my substance use and the other was an irrational thinking problem.

The Solution

The answers will come, if your own house is in order.

—Big Book of Alcoholics Anonymous

Our continuing spiritual growth through the program has given us solutions to the problems we thought we couldn't solve. Through disciplined concentration on the Twelve Steps and working the program, the answers have come, some slowly, some quickly.

One solution was the change in our attitude when we admitted and accepted the seriousness of our addiction. This awakening prompted the willingness to begin working the Twelve Steps. The answer is the development of honesty, gratitude, faith, belief, humility, and the ability to love others and our inner self.

My recovery is physical, mental, emotional, and spiritual. When I am willing to work on all four, the answers will come.

Grace

But for the grace of God, there go I.
—John Bradford

When we come in contact with those who have not yet found the program, our first reaction is one of relief and gratitude. "There but for the grace of God, go I," we think. The next reaction is "How can I help them find what I've found?"

Before we began recovery, we would have traded in our lives for almost anyone else's. Now after a time on the program, we feel differently about ourselves. We hear people giving thanks for their disease. They tell us without their disease they wouldn't have found the program, and without the program they wouldn't have found recovery.

We quit our addiction before, and it never produced this sense of well-being. The difference is the program, the fellowship, and our connection with a Higher Power.

Whatever it was that brought me to the program,
I have learned to be thankful for it. As I come
in contact with those who still suffer, I can never
forget that if it weren't for the grace of God,
I would be where they are today.

Believing

I came; I came to; I came to believe.
—Anonymous

We hear repeatedly that belief is acceptance of truths without proof. We are always tempted to demand proof. God has granted us logic, and we think we are expected to use it. And we are, except when it comes to proving God's existence. Then we are expected to act in faith. Many of us began to use our Higher Power before we began to understand it.

Proof is sometimes tricky. For instance, after we hear terrifying stories from those who decide to try using again, we don't have to follow their example in order to prove them right or wrong. We can trust their experience.

The only proof we need that the program works is to look around at the old-timers in our fellowship and to listen to their stories of the way it was and the way it is now.

Faith in the recovery power of the Steps keeps me mindful that one of them begins "came to believe." Unless I maintain my belief and faith in the Steps, I am in danger of suffering a relapse.

Surrender

I can't . . . God can . . . I think I'll let Him.

—Anonymous

We have all lived with the idea we could do anything. We have seen spaceships sent to outer planets. We can send a message across continents in a moment. How, then, do we come to terms with our limitations? How do we teach ourselves to say, "I can't"? Where do we learn to trust our limitations and believe that God can take us places we cannot take ourselves?

Our program tells us to stop trying to manage the world. We will never be all things to all people. Our whole trouble was the misuse of willpower. When we lower our expectations, we are not setting our sights on lower goals. We are surrendering ourselves to our Higher Power. We are asking help to be better than we are.

I need to remember that "surrender" doesn't mean "give up." It means admitting to my Higher Power that I need help to reach my goals.

No Free Ride

The elevator is broken; use the Steps.
—Anonymous

Elevators are easy. We push a button, and we go right to the top. The way is fast, quick, and silent. We don't work up a sweat. We don't get out of breath. We can't trip and fall. There is not much time to communicate with anyone else along the way, so we don't have to use any effort or thought. We can daydream as we face the front of the car and stare at the numbers as they change from floor to floor.

Then the elevator breaks, and we crash to the ground. Those of us who survive are told to take the Steps to get where we want to go. Our addictions were our elevators out of living. The substance-induced highs we experienced were just like an elevator ride. Until we crashed.

I will sometimes sweat, stumble, get out of breath in my climb, but I'll take the time to talk with and learn from others who are taking the Steps with me.

Prejudice

There is a principle which is a bar against all information . . . and which cannot fail to keep [us] in everlasting ignorance—that principle is contempt prior to investigation.

—Herbert Spencer

When we were introduced to the program, we were full of prejudices. We thought the members were some sort of religious cult, that they were a bunch of freaks, that they were self-righteous quitters who just couldn't handle their use, that they didn't know what they were talking about, that they couldn't possibly have had the problems we had because they all looked so happy.

Then the members started to speak. What they said and how they said it showed us immediately that we had prejudged them. They were spiritual, not religious; they had been where we were; they knew what they were talking about; they still had problems but they were handling them. We began to want what they had. Our prejudices began to be removed.

I am learning to wait and see what the truth is instead of relying on old ideas and prejudices I once held.

Quiet Time

Each morning sees some task begun.
Each evening sees it done. Something
attempted, something done.

—Henry Wadsworth Longfellow

Every day for us is a period of spiritual growth. Restful sleep prepares us for fruitful days. As each day begins, a new adventure in growth lies ahead. We seek strength and an attitude of making our lives more meaningful and positive through prayer and meditation at the start of each new day during our quiet time. We prepare ourselves emotionally for the busy hours ahead.

With positive action planned ahead, we arise to a day dedicated to accomplishment. We know we have little time for standing and idly staring. We accept new challenges as we carry out each day's plans. We encourage those around us to join us in seeking to see the best in everything that makes up our daily lives.

Restful sleep, meditation, planning,
and turning it over starts my day with
a quiet time and keeps it manageable.

No Regrets

Of all sad words of tongue or pen, the saddest are these, 'It might have been.'

—John Greenleaf Whittier

Unless we live in the *now*, we are in danger of suffering the agony of regret. We can't spend all our time thinking "life's not fair." We cannot afford to excuse everything with "what ifs?" We used those words constantly during the years we wasted on obeying compulsions we knew could destroy us.

We remember the years before recovery and accept them as object lessons of what it could be like again if we become careless or complacent. But we don't regret them. Regret only leads to depression and perhaps a return to active addiction.

We must stop dwelling on the impossibility of undoing the wrongs of yesterday. Instead, we must begin enjoying the "right things" that are now possible in recovery.

It is impossible to relive my past. I can only create a good past now by living this day the best way I can, so that tomorrow I can look back without having to say, "It might have been."

First Things First

Do not climb the hill until you get to it.
—English saying

As each day goes by, we gain a clearer perspective on our lives. We realize that our recovery program is our most important priority. Our sponsor and home group are ever-present reminders to keep "First things first." We never stray too far from our First Step. We remember that when we came into the program we were flat on our backs. Before we could crawl, we had to learn to sit up. Before we could walk, we had to learn to stand. There is no alternative to doing "First things first."

Our meetings help us to shut off the voices that tell us to solve tomorrow's problems today. We pray and meditate on the things that are directly in front of us. When we own the present, we have peace of mind. When we rent the future, we buy trouble.

If I make the proper preparations and wait until I get there to climb the hill, the climb is easier.

• JULY 19 •

Humility

The Twelve Step way of life is humble, not necessarily meek.

—*Anonymous*

The picture many of us get of a humble person is someone afraid of their own shadow, whose self-image is so low they're afraid to stand up for themselves. We learn that this image of humility is not what is meant in the program. We realize that the people who have stayed abstinent for some time are all humble.

For those who have made progress in the program, humility is simply a clear recognition of what and who they are. They have gotten down to their own right size. Humility is understanding that they're worthwhile. It's the middle ground between the extremes of grandiosity and intense shame. They have a sincere desire to be and become the best they can be.

Today I will remember that humility is not being meek. It's being me. Humility for me means staying my "right size."

Acceptance

The Twelve Step way of life is accepting, not necessarily passive.

—Anonymous

When we accept life on life's terms, we are acknowledging reality. We have all, on occasion, run from the truth. When we were in a situation that frightened us, we would turn tail and run. We would do our imitation of an ostrich and stick our heads in the sand, pretending the situation didn't exist and was not happening.

When we *accept* something, we are not passively taking it in. We are ready to work through and toward our new awareness. But we can't do anything at all unless we accept it as a reality.

We know what it's like to run from our disease. We tried to prove it was anything and everything but addiction. We tried to prove it was caused by something wrong in our lives our jobs, our family, our childhood, our relationships, even the weather. After we ran out of excuses, we finally accepted our disease.

My acceptance of my addiction is not passive, but based in reality and truth.

Love

The Twelve Step way of life is loving, not necessarily possessing.

—*Anonymous*

When a practicing addict or alcoholic loves someone, it is not usually love that is transmitted. It's more like taking hostages. Just as our contact with a Higher Power was blocked by the disease, so also was our contact with loved ones blocked. While we were preoccupied with addiction, we could only hold on for dear life.

The expression of love turned into either a possessive hold or detached emotional unavailability. Either way, the practicing addict did not make a good lover. The disease itself was a jealous suitor. It demanded a total, unconditional commitment.

When we began to recover, our ability to love returned, or was born within us for the first time. Love has become a key to an ever-growing spiritual life and a newfound ability to commit and bond.

My Step work has helped me become less possessive and self-centered, and capable of loving relationships.

Honesty

The Twelve Step way of life is honest,
not necessarily self-righteous.

—*Anonymous*

When we allowed ourselves to drift from the real world, it was often a difficult experience to find a way back. It caused deep pain and guilt. When we confronted our life history in our Fourth Step, we found that we had to go back to the very beginning to find our way home. The trip wasn't easy, but it had to be made if we were to get on with our lives.

After we began cleaning up the wreckage of our past, we made every effort to be honest daily. Now inventory taking is gentle, with soft edges. We remember how hard it was for us to come clean, and we have sympathy for those who still face this test. We guard against being righteous in our dealings with others. We do not want to wear our honesty on our sleeves. We should not be proud that we have become honest. Honesty should be as natural for us as breathing.

When I am self-righteous in my approach to others,
I am not being honest; I am just being mean.

• JULY 23 •

Honor

The Twelve Step way of life is honorable, not necessarily prideful.

—*Anonymous*

A proud air serves no purpose for a person in recovery, other than being a warning flag to all. Proud people fall hard. Honorable and humble people are so close to the ground they can't fall. When we are too proud, we act self-righteous. Self-righteousness says we know more than anyone else, and we are out to push that point. All we really know is what we experience in our recovery. We can contribute nothing more than truth. Everything else is opinion.

When we become prideful about our experience, we look like fools, for all of us make mistakes. When we are full of pride about our opinions, we act crazy, because they all too often take us on fantasy rides into the land of nowhere.

I am to be humble in all my affairs. Humility teaches me I can be honorable and honest. This will bring honor to my life, love to my heart, and peace to my soul.

Enviable

The Twelve Step way of life is enviable, not necessarily smug.

—*Anonymous*

We have many moments in our recovery when we close our eyes and wonder how could we be so lucky and so blessed. There is no question that life in recovery is very different from the life before it. What we could not achieve on our own, we now can achieve through the Steps. We have a sense of having made it. We have found what others are still striving for. At times we do feel special and maybe just a little smug.

It is true we are in an enviable position. We have become happier through a most unlikely journey. The disease that cost us the most is now the means to our serenity. We hear people speak with gratitude about their disease, and we know exactly what they mean.

I am reminded that I have what I have by no power of my own. It is the grace of my Higher Power that has brought me to the fellowship.

Spiritual

The Twelve Step way of life is spiritual, not necessarily religious.

—Anonymous

The journey to spirituality does not pass through any particular religious tradition. The spiritual life we speak of in recovery is not about the adoption of ceremony or conversion to a certain kind of organized thinking. Spirituality has to do with the quality of our relationship to whatever or whomever is most important in our life.

We come to the spiritual through our discovery of a Power *other* than ourselves. This Power is not something over which we have any personal control. We can only identify it as higher than we are. As we continue to work the Steps, our experience with our Higher Power grows. We trust the influence this Power has over our lives. Many of us feel comfortable calling this Power God. Some will continue their journey back into a particular religion.

Spirituality found within the program is not religious. Each individual in recovery comes to terms with their own spirit-life in their own way, as I have come to terms with mine.

Attractive

The Twelve Step way of life is attractive, not necessarily irresistible.

—*Anonymous*

Life looks different through rose-colored glasses. Everything has beautiful shades and hues. We see every person as prettier or handsomer than they actually are. When we look in the mirror, the mole on our nose is smaller. The padded hips and double chin disappear. By some strange force, we look three inches taller.

We should all be permitted the use of these glasses once in a while. The newcomer, especially, needs the chance to pick up their spirits. Early recovery can feel irresistible, like those rose-colored glasses. The truth of the matter is we have learned the Twelve Step way of life is attractive, but not irresistible.

I have come to appreciate how attractive my new life is. I no longer need to use rose-colored glasses all the time to view my world.

Confusion

Lord Ronald . . . flung himself upon his horse and rode madly away in all directions.

— *Stephen Leacock*

Before the program, we were like Lord Ronald. We flung ourselves upon our addiction and rode madly away in all directions and into many strange mental states. This included frightening, impulsive behavior while in a blackout. Those who had blackouts were in complete disbelief when told of the wild and incredible things they did.

Sometimes the addict is conscious of how they are behaving and either does not care or is unable to resist acting that way. Loved ones, close friends, and coworkers frequently become concerned and frightened by the confused state of someone "under the influence." The worst reaction of others is an acceptance of "confused" states of the addict as "it's something they can't help" or "there's no use trying to help the helpless."

The confusion I created when I was using was harmful to everyone, especially me. That confusion has now been thankfully replaced with clarity.

Self-Conquest

If I were given the opportunity to present a gift to the next generation it would be the ability of each individual to learn to laugh at himself.
—*Charles Schultz*

In recovery, we learn to laugh at the kind of person we were when our addiction was out of control. We don't laugh at the fact of our addiction; we laugh at who we once were. This is a healthy kind of self-ridicule. Above all, we laugh at the person we never again have to be if we follow the principles of our program. To blot out the "me" of yesterday, we have only to follow some very simple guidelines.

At times, obeying the principles that have been set down for us may not be easy. But with our realization that we have chosen to stop playing God comes the awareness that difficulties need not be disastrous. If everything in life came easily, we would lack sparkle in our lives.

I am thankful my sense of humor has found freedom. Now I am able to laugh at myself, which is the height of self-conquest.

Opportunities

A wise man will make more
opportunities than he finds.
—Francis Bacon

Opportunities are like miracles in our life of recovery. But they won't necessarily fall into our hands without any effort on our part. Spiritual progress is the self-chosen goal we seek in our recovery. Opportunities for spiritual progress are abundant in the program. We have a positive attitude that comes from working all the Steps.

Opportunities for growth are earned, not given. When we work to make opportunities happen, we can enjoy the success that follows, not only for ourselves, but for others. Admitting our powerlessness gave us the freedom of choice, the freedom for opportunities.

In recovery, I delight in the chance I have to make my own successes through planned progress instead of simply wishing for the best things in life.

Giving Up

There must be a beginning of any great matter but the continuing unto the end until it is fully finished yields the true glory.

— *Sir Francis Drake*

It isn't a matter of stubbornness to persist in any effort. It is common sense. When we persist in taking our time and carefully consider how to handle a situation or give an answer, we usually discover the right solution. We spent most of our lives before the program always "giving up."

It's easy to give up on a problem too quickly. A lengthy effort at finding a solution is sometimes painful and irritating. But the answers will come if we continue doing the research through study and prayer, one day at a time.

When we decide to begin a kind act, we may need bulldog determination to follow that act to its completion. We should enter into any action with a strong desire. There can be no hesitation or any thought of hanging back in taking the correct action toward answers.

The road may be long and hard before I find the answers. I will not give up too quickly.

Closed Mind

When your head begins to swell,
your mind stops growing.
—*Anonymous*

In the old days before recovery, we knew everything. We could talk for hours about any topic, whether we knew anything about it or not. Our minds were closed to new information because it might shatter what little confidence we had in ourselves. We knew what we knew, and that was enough.

In recovery, we know that we don't know everything. What a relief! We learn something new every day, and we never seem to get enough. The world is an exciting place full of new discoveries. And it's okay to say "I don't know," because then we can open our minds and hearts to the answer.

My confidence has grown, so I don't have to
pretend that I know everything any more.
Now I have the courage to open my mind
and learn without getting a swelled head
by being overconfident.

Growth

Growth itself contains the germ of happiness.
—Pearl S. Buck

When we're out of sorts with everyone and everything, and we realize that we're the one who needs to change, that's growth.

When we mind our own business and don't take the inventory of another, that's growth.

When we don't expect anyone to change their opinion simply because it differs from ours, that's growth.

When we think we're right at one moment then are proven wrong the next, and are happy about it because we've learned something, that's growth.

When we are as happy about another's progress as we are about our own, that's growth.

When we welcome each new day instead of dreading it, that's growth.

I used to seek happiness in material things
and overdependence on other people.
Now growth itself is happiness.

Self-Confidence

Every day, in every way, I am getting better and better.

—Émile Coué

If our program were made up of men and women who kept telling others and themselves, "I'm no good, I'll never make it," the program itself could never survive. We win only when we have confidence in our own capabilities and limitations. We sincerely believe that, with a shared feeling of love among our members, success is not only possible but guaranteed.

Years ago, people around the world made fun of the phrase about getting better and better. Despite all the belittlement, that expression of confidence helped many to a more healthful life. It still works. We know that if we do not have faith in ourselves, no one else will. We can always choose to be our own best friend rather than our own worst enemy.

I've heard it said, "We are what we are."
Self-confidence in my ability to make
spiritual growth can achieve wonders.
I am getting better and better.

Caretaking

Don't care FOR, care ABOUT.
—Anonymous

When we care *for* someone, we are letting that person be the focus of our lives. We take over the decisions and responsibilities for that person. We can bond with someone a lot better than with their needs. When we care *about* someone, we are concerned about their journey. We nurture, encourage, and support them on their way.

Many of us have to learn to give up playing the role of caretaker with people. We have been a one-person Humane Society, moving from place to place, picking up stray dogs and cats. We are told that caretaking is an improper response to our need to be accepted.

Whatever the reason we play the role, it is not helpful to continue in recovery. We need to let people care for their own needs. Everyone should have the opportunity to love themselves.

I learn that caring FOR someone will probably cause the relationship to fail. Caring ABOUT them will allow the relationship and the person to succeed.

Serenity

There is a gentle serenity in God's peace; there is a soothing tranquility in God's love.

—*Anonymous*

The words *gentle* and *soothing* can quiet the most troubled heart. The notion of serenity and tranquility can create an inner peace that is wonderful. What good is it if a person owns the entire world and does not have serenity and tranquility? What have our hearts cried out for from the time we took our first breath if not for serenity and tranquility? When we speak of hopes and dreams, we are talking of finding serenity and tranquility.

In Step Three we found them. Once we made a decision to turn our will and our lives over to the care of a Higher Power, we render ourselves open to the gentle serenity of God's peace and the soothing tranquility of God's love.

The Serenity Prayer starts "God grant . . ." Serenity is a gift that God grants. When I take my will out of the way in Step Three, then God can grant me serenity.

Recovery Tools

Man is a tool-using animal. . . . Without tools he is nothing, with tools he is all.

—Thomas Carlyle

When we hear, "You alone can make it happen, but you can't do it alone," we are being told, among other bits of advice, that we need tools in addition to the people who share our problems and solutions. The tools for recovery are many, and they are simple in form and made for simple usage. Basically, the primary tools are the Twelve Steps of our program.

Among our most dependable tools is the freedom to accept our problems. This tool is the one that starts us on our journey through the Steps. It helps us turn our will over to God after we have decided that a Higher Power can restore us to sanity. Each Step is a tool, helping us go through inventories, make amends, improve our conscious contact with God, and understand our Higher Power's will for us.

I have learned which recovery tool to use at a particular time. And I continue to increase my desire and my ability to use each tool properly.

God's Will

You are exactly where God wants you to be.

—Anonymous

When we took our First Step, we admitted we were powerless over our disease. This single admission opened us up to a bigger realization: we just might not be in charge of *anything*. We were also powerless over people, places, and things. When we recognized this, a different future became ours. We came to believe that our Higher Power was in charge. We did not have to know the plan before it was revealed. We could trust that we would be well cared for, always.

There are still times when we feel insecure and uneasy about our lives. At those times, we may question God. We may wonder if we're being punished for something we've done wrong. We may ask if this is all there is to recovery. We can hold fast to the truth that we are just where God would have us.

The times I take control and attempt to force a change will only cause me to lose touch with my Higher Power. I will be patient. I believe answers will emerge at exactly the right time.

Fearing the Unknown

The actual enemy is the unknown.
—Thomas Mann

Before we entered the program, fear of the unknown was a large part of our lives. After a time in recovery, we learn how to control that fear by controlling our tendency to return to old behavior or use of harmful substances.

We know that recovery based wholly on fear will not last. If we spend all our time being afraid of our addiction, we won't be able to enjoy the changes and discoveries of our new life. We function better on common sense. Our understanding of fear needs to be based in reality. We thrive on trust rather than worry, uncertainty, and dread.

We are taught that we don't need to fear the unknown when we learn to turn it over to our Higher Power. The unknown becomes simply a chance to change for the better.

Much of my fear of the unknown springs from my lack of confidence in coping with unexpected experiences. I am learning to live without anticipating trouble and to deal with it when it comes.

• AUGUST 8 •

Thirteenth Step

The Thirteenth Step is taken by members who suffer from the delusion that sex can cure their addiction.

—*Anonymous*

Both women and men practice the selfish Thirteenth Step. They're not always easy to spot. Some go to meetings and appear to work the program, while others just sit around clubhouses, eyeballing others they desire (always newcomers), waiting their chance to pounce. Newcomers, being somewhat bewildered, sometimes confuse lust with love and fall victim to this dangerous game.

Many newcomers have run from the program when they realize the "help" being offered was a mask for sexual favors. Many of these unsuspecting newcomers never come back. Sex has never cured anyone's obsessions or addictions.

I am responsible for not using my experience in the program to take advantage of a fellow member, especially a newcomer. If I see anyone Thirteenth Stepping, I will do what I can to tell the person how unlucky the Thirteenth Step is.

God's Gifts

God will never give you more than you can handle.

—Anonymous

There were times before we began our recovery that a trip to the store was too much for us. As time went on, we could handle less and less. Our addiction had made the simplest tasks unmanageable. The more we relied on ourselves, the more we were let down. We became the ultimate of basket cases.

Now, in recovery, we have opened to a Power that takes care of all our concerns. We are asked to take certain Steps and work our program. Satisfaction comes in knowing that God will never give us more than we can handle. We soon realize that we can handle much more than we thought.

Our temptation is to slip back into our old patterns when things get complicated. We used to think we could hide from our troubles. Now we trust in God and allow our Higher Power to work for us.

In time, simple solutions appear. Calmness returns. I don't need to fear change or problems.

A Selfish Program

A person shows their true self by how much they need other people.

—Anonymous

What giving we have discovered in our fellowship! From the very first meeting, we received an outstretched hand that offered us help. People gave freely and asked nothing in return. We, who had known so much taking, could hardly believe what we experienced. It just didn't seem real.

The reality is no put-on. There is a spirit of selfless fellowship in our program. But the truth is that those who are giving are also keeping. The gem they are holding onto is their recovery. Only those who give away what they have found can keep it.

Every time we share with another human being, we add something to our spiritual bank account, allowing us to draw on it when extra demands are made upon our courage. In sharing our burdens, they become lighter.

Imagine people saving their lives by giving them away! Oh, that I can only be so selfish!

King or Queen Baby

The first 30 years of my childhood nearly killed me.

—Anonymous

King or Queen Baby attitudes and behavior are a block to recovery. Many of us have carried into our adult lives childish egos and immature attitudes. We won't give up our child-like needs of control or our desire that all our needs be met. An attitude of *I want what I want when I want it*, and motives of power, attention, and instant pleasure have no place in our program.

Recovery teaches us ways to deal with our scared little child and at the same time allows us to nurture the child within us all. When we act like babies, we think we are the center of the world, and believe that status, fame, money, and beauty are the most important things in life. When we admitted defeat, we needed to put our childish behavior behind us. We changed from believing in "baby power" to believing in a Higher Power.

I will continue to put away my babyish behavior by working on self-discovery, self-acceptance, self-discipline, and self-forgiveness.

The Bright Side

You grow up the day you have your first real laugh at yourself.

—Ethel Barrymore

One of the most popular identifications of how important laughter is to members of the fellowship is that "laughter is the best medicine." So many of us lived only on the dark side of life before the program. We experienced healing when we were able to lighten up and laugh.

We often wanted to cry bitterly over what we had become. But we pretended to the world that everything was fine by laughing at everything, being sarcastic, and making a joke out of even the worst things we did. We were afraid that if we started to cry, we'd never stop.

In recovery, we find we don't have to struggle to avoid shedding tears. Those tears come from humility, trust, joy, and faith. And we can laugh with gratitude over the changes we find in ourselves and in those we have come to love.

I am no longer afraid to laugh or cry.
I am able to accept myself as human.

Reality

Realities are far less dangerous than fantasies.
—Anonymous

When we speak of being restored to sanity, we could well be speaking of restoring reality to our lives. Our addictions, compulsions, and dependencies kept us in a world of weird fantasy. Mental extremes made us think and feel unnaturally.

When intoxicated or "high," everything weird seemed to "belong," to be real and natural. The fantasy we accepted was from the realm of insanity. We accepted "fate" as our lot, but when the haze of the unreal left, we often experienced shame, guilt, and regret from knowing what we had accepted.

As we found recovery and escaped the shackles of addiction, we came to realize that spiritual growth was not as hopeless for us as our experiences had led us to believe. But we had to reach for reality and reject what was fantasy. Change comes when recovery removes all of the confusion from our dream world of addiction.

Reality never changes, but my acceptance of it does. The real world is very different from the impression my addiction gave me.

Sponsors

Call your sponsor before, not after,
you take your first drink.
—*Anonymous*

Sponsors are those who have experienced the benefits of the program. They are willing to help us on our journey because they know the road we are traveling. They tell us to slow down when we need to, and answer our questions: "How long will I feel guilty? How important is doing Steps Four and Five? When will I get over these drunk dreams? When do I get some serenity?"

When we came into the program, many of us thought we only needed to stay abstinent. Then we heard that we needed to change other aspects of our life, and most of us didn't like it a bit. We asked our sponsor what needed to be changed. The sponsor said "You only need to change three things." We were relieved, until our sponsor continued, "Everything you say, everything you think, and everything you do."

When my sponsor told me to change only three things, he smiled. I didn't. I do now.

The "Yets"

Nothing is so bad that relapse won't make it worse.

—Anonymous

The stories we hear in meetings often shock us. It seems hard to believe that some members could have harmed themselves in such ways. We hear about arrests, bankruptcies, loss of family and home, lost jobs, violence, jail, physical injury—the list goes on. Most of us said to ourselves, "I never was that bad. Maybe I don't really belong here."

Our sponsors and fellow members quickly straightened us out. We were *comparing* our histories with other members. We were told to *identify* with the stories, not compare. Some of us had been lucky that worse things hadn't happened to us while we were using. We were reminded those things hadn't happened to us *yet*. If we relapsed, the "yets" were waiting.

Today I'll remember to identify not compare. I don't want to relapse and go through the "yets."

Trust

Our entire program rests on the principle of mutual trust. We trust our Higher Power, we trust the program, and we trust each other.

—*Anonymous*

When we were using, we trusted no one. We lied about everything, even the smallest thing, so how could we trust what anyone else told us? Cheating was a way of life. Finding reasons for our actions kept us busy rationalizing away our lives.

So how could we trust anyone? How could we trust ourselves? We couldn't even trust ourselves to keep track of our lies. They were so big and so many and so confusing that we just drowned our denial in substances. Then it didn't matter anymore.

The only thing we thought we could trust was our addiction. When we discovered it was the biggest lie of all, we lost trust in everything. We had nowhere to go. And that was the greatest day of our lives.

I have put my trust in the program, the Steps, my sponsor, my group, and my Higher Power, and, little by little, day by day, I am learning to trust again.

Prayer

The only way to pray is to pray, and the way to pray well is to pray often.

—Anonymous

To us in recovery, prayer is always the one great move on our part that leads to spiritual progress. The need for prayer and meditation is a big part of our program. Step Eleven is centered on the necessity for us to seek through prayer and meditation our own awareness of what God's will is for us.

We now know that prayer is best when it takes the form of a conversation with our Higher Power. Surely it can never be a span of time during which we are engaged only in asking, demanding, bargaining, or borrowing. A large part of all prayer and meditation should be devoted to our listening for answers. And answers do always come to those who are patient, tolerant, and trusting.

When I began to pray in recovery, the only prayer I said was "Thank You, God." Now I have many other prayers and I pray often. Now I know that my prayers are answered.

Lying

What a tangled web we weave when first we practice to deceive.
— William Shakespeare

When we set out to lie, the person always most painfully hurt is ourself. Trying to fool people is always done with arrogance. "You can't fool all the people all the time." This deprives us of the ability to be willing and open-minded. These lost qualities are necessary for us to have within ourselves if we are to find a comfortable recovery.

Both big and white lies seldom go undetected by the people in contact with the liar. Dishonesty always leads to the knowledge that the dishonest one is a cheat. This results in a return of painful shame, guilt, and regret.

The program reminds us that those who cannot or will not recover are incapable of being completely honest with themselves.

I know that my lies are dishonest. The program suggests to me that absolute honesty is impossible for humans but I have the capacity to grow in honesty.

Asking for Help

The smartest thing a Twelve Step member can say is "help me."
—Anonymous

The weight of carrying the world on our backs has been removed from us in recovery. It is good to remember the world was never ours to carry in the first place. Our program prevents us from setting ourselves up for failure. Most of us are used to being the Lone Ranger. Instead of silver bullets, we left empty lives. Our solitude taught us never to ask for help, always to go it alone. Our isolation produced a pitiful figure we would dress up in toughness.

This, of course, was phony, because inside we were anything but tough. When we operate alone, pretending to be strong and in control, we set ourselves in motion to experience depression and pain. "Stinking thinking" flourishes in isolation. The key to unlocking the many gifts of the fellowship is asking for help. There is strength, wisdom, and hope, all waiting for us if we ask for help.

I have learned to ask for help and to help when I am asked.

Common Sense

We are what we think. All that we are arises with our thoughts. With our thoughts we make our world.
—Buddha

Common sense is a good approach to living in our recovery program. Step Ten of our program states that it is wise to pause often to analyze all our choices. Hurried remarks or actions can lead to errors. We learn that, when we are wrong, we promptly admit it.

That admission, of course, reflects honesty and humility at their very best. We grow in understanding and effectiveness. A hasty remark or behavior can injure or anger the person at whom it is directed. All too often, this results in embarrassment and hurt. Our responsibility to carry the message does not entitle us to "ram it down the throats" of even those we think badly need our advice.

I should always think before I act or speak. Common sense reminds me that "to know what I know and to know what I don't know is knowing what it's all about."

Reading

Reading makes a complete person.

—Anonymous

When humans first found a way to turn spoken words into symbols, knowledge became available to untold numbers.

Through carvings on stone and scribblings on parchment, a method of communication became available to all who truly cared to learn. The simplest of words were used in the first efforts to teach humans.

Simplicity is still the recommended way of working a recovery program. We both read and hear that the program is "simple—though not always easy."

Reading, study, and meditation can give us the basis of wisdom. The knowledge we gain from reading helps us understand ourselves and our world better. The wisdom we gather from books helps us on our journey of recovery.

The fogginess and lack of concentration I had when I first started recovery has faded away. Reading has become an important part of my program.

Responsibility

I am responsible for myself; my recovery, my well-being, my happiness, all these things are, ultimately, my own responsibility.

—*Anonymous*

We are responsible.

Our Higher Power does not lay claim to our free will. We can choose not to be responsible and make ourselves more miserable by going to new levels of despair and depression. Or we can seize every opportunity for a better life.

When we were newcomers and just getting started, we were generally very confused. We welcomed the support. Many of us were fed up with our lives and would have freely turned them in for a different model. But we learned to put into action what we were learning.

Our sponsors give us good advice and sound instructions. We can choose to listen to the advice or not.

Although we will always be dependent on God for our strength, it is up to us to ask God for that strength and do the necessary work to receive it.

Today I'll remember my Higher Power has given me free will to accept or reject responsibility. My life is better when I act responsibly.

Quiet Times

Listen to the sounds of silence.
—Paul Simon

Sharing experiences, strengths, and hopes, and reading during recovery is very important. But just as important are the times of silence we allow ourselves to think over the information we're receiving during times of sharing and reading.

Before recovery, being quiet may have meant having to face our problems alone. We avoided being by ourselves. We may think we don't have time for silence in our busy lives. But quiet moments in the morning or evening for meditation, moments going to and from work, moments spent doing household chores, moments during exercise—all of these moments add up to the precious times of silence we need to absorb all we are learning, feeling, and experiencing.

I now look forward to my quiet times.
I am learning how to relax and be with
my Higher Power in prayer, meditation,
and reflection.

Meetings

Seven days without a meeting makes one weak.

—Anonymous

The amount of time we invested in our addiction over the years was considerable. We spent countless hours feeding our addiction, thinking about feeding it, and trying to recover from the episode. A great investment of time was made.

We need to consider the idea that a tremendous amount of time invested in recovery is a wise choice. This disease of ours has deep wounds. Healing will take time. Just because we put the substance or behavior down does not mean they will put us down. Our program describes them as cunning, baffling, and powerful. Some old-timers add patient, too.

The point is made in many cases that those who don't spend the time, don't make it. Ours is not a solitary fellowship. We don't work our program alone. The meetings we attend are very important to us.

I will put as much energy into my meeting attendance as I once put into my active addiction.

Self-Centeredness

Self-love is the greatest of all flatterers.
—François de La Rochefoucauld

Those who follow the principles of the program have learned that self-centeredness is possibly one of their biggest problems. Since we come to believe that we cannot succeed in staying abstinent by our own efforts alone, we realize that self-idolizing is the worst possible tool to make vital friendships. There is little doubt that thinking "me above all" will make us inhabitants of glass houses that are always in danger of being shattered.

Selfishness and loneliness are created by an oversupply of concern for who we are and what we will be. Selfishness and self-centeredness lead to a complete failure in working the program. We are encouraged in recovery to become *other-centered*, thus getting our minds off ourselves.

When my ego causes me to indulge in
self-flattery, let me remember that when
I fall in love with myself, I won't have
any rivals for my affection.

Today Is the Now

I've shut the door on yesterday
And thrown the key away.
Tomorrow holds no fears for me
Since I have found today.
— Vivian Y. Laramore

Living in the now is one of the most important ways of finding lasting recovery. One of the favorite slogans to be followed is "One day at a time." We willingly accept the fact that yesterday is gone forever and tomorrow is only an expectation. When we have finished with yesterday and have no fear of tomorrow, we can be assured that we can truly be content with each new today.

Living in the now is an acceptance of life's realities. Honesty is the key to being happy throughout each day as it comes. Today surely is the "first day of the rest of our lives." It can be, if lived with gratitude, love, and honesty, the best day yet in our newly found today.

Today truly can be that wonderful exciting day
that on yesterday I eagerly called "tomorrow."
I can greet every today by exclaiming, "This day
can be the start of the best years of my life."

Perfectionism

Accept me as I am, so that I may
learn what I can become.

—*Anonymous*

Most of us have lived our lives trying to be perfect. We couldn't tolerate mistakes in our lives or those around us. We expected everything to be perfect. We tried to control everything. We would not do things because they wouldn't turn out perfect, which left us not doing anything except standing still. We were always afraid of being criticized.

We were always setting high, unrealistic goals. When failure came, we became frustrated, angry, and depressed. We felt inadequate.

We have been allowed to have a different view in recovery. We give up trying to be perfect. We work at being human, not godlike as our addiction led us to believe. We remember the program tells us, "We're not saints. Progress, not perfection."

I am less and less trapped by grandiosity
and perfectionism. This allows me to be
human and learn from my mistakes.

Think, Think, Think

To know what you know and to know what you don't know is knowing what it's all about.

—*Anonymous*

When we work our program, we are reintroduced to a person about whom we knew very little and understood not at all. This person was ourselves. We traced our personal histories back in time and discovered the many ways our addictions were living our lives. They walked for us, talked for us, cried for us, ate for us, made love for us, and on many occasions, tried to murder us. This power overwhelmed us. It wasn't until we began our recovery that we discovered a way out.

We have been given our lives back. We are now in possession of all our senses and skills. However, they have not been used much; they are rusty. We need to practice being ourselves. The slogan "Think, think, think" reminds us that what we tell ourselves affects our actions.

I must remember to "Think, think, think" before I act, react, or pursue my desires.

Teachers

To teach is to learn twice over.
—Joseph Joubert

At every meeting, there is an abundance of teachers, ready, willing, and able to pass on to others the results of lessons they have experienced through constant open-minded attendance at meetings. New arrivals to a group frequently hear, "Find a teacher, and you will find a new friend."

This truism is soon apparent to any who choose to listen to teachers. The passing on to others of the useful lessons learned in recovery comes from those members who have savored recovery for lengths of time ranging from a few months to several decades.

Beginners readily accept the advice they receive because one of the first realizations a newcomer enjoys is that they are hearing honesty. He or she knows they can believe what they hear and will never have to take the painful steps of learning facts from personal experience.

I have met many teachers in my recovery.
They hold the torches that light the way for me
to learn. I will continue to follow the light.

Winners

Stick with the winners.

—Anonymous

We came to the program with different opinions about who were the winners. Some of us thought a fat bank account meant winning. Others looked to how little one had lost before coming into the program as criteria for winning. There are those who are smart, some pretty, others with good jobs. We discover rather quickly that winning has nothing to do with how one appears to be or what one has.

Winning is about how one *lives*. Therefore, we want to watch the men and women who have had time in the program. We don't look for just birthday numbers. We watch how the Steps have been and are being worked. We look for the men and women who exhibit humility, gratitude, and spirituality. The winners are usually the ones involved in service. They understand that to keep what they have, they must give it away. The winners freely share their experience, strength, and hope with all of us.

I want to stick with the winners. If I do,
the winners will stick with me.

Patience

Our patience will achieve
more than our force.
—Edmund Burke

"Easy does it" is a slogan and a philosophy of all Twelve Step groups. Those who seek success in the program are advised to resist being hasty and to be willing to wait. When we mature and solutions to our problems appear, we can take action. Then who we are and what we do will be lasting.

Waiting patiently and carefully is not procrastinating. Every moment we spend learning is an investment in the knowledge that we have found the right answers.

Self-doubt can cause us to put things off. But all we need is to be willing to turn it over to our Higher Power. Accepting this does not mean that we rush blindly into action. It means we also become willing to wait for our Higher Power's direction in all things. Waiting or even just having a willingness to wait *is* action.

I'm no longer rushing around in the fast lane.
With acceptance and willingness, I can now
tell the difference between what is and
what is not. "Easy does it."

SEPTEMBER

Live and Let Live

No matter how it feels, we're moving forward. No matter how good it gets, the best is yet to come.

—*Anonymous*

It is hard to live more than one life at a time. Try as we did to organize everyone's life according to our plan, it just didn't work. We learned in our First Step that we were not masters of the universe, that our very best efforts got us into the program. We had to file away the little manager in our heads that found it necessary to bark out all the orders to God.

Once we did, and took our rightful place as just a fellow traveler on the road to recovery, we finally began to live and allow others the opportunity to live.

Live and let live is a simple idea that, when practiced, produces lasting results, more serenity, and peace of mind. It permits us to turn over our self-assumed responsibility for other people's lives to our Higher Power. And what a relief that is!

Live and let live is the Twelve Step way of life.
When I live my own life and let others live theirs,
I am letting go and letting God be in charge.

Understanding

I shall light a candle of understanding in thine heart which shall not be put out.

—Apocrypha

When we found an understanding of the disease that made us captives to addiction, we came to a realization of both our problem and the solution. But we needed to fully understand. There could be no guesswork. If some experienced relapses, we could acknowledge the fact that their understanding was not complete. As spiritual progress continues, we become more and more certain that there is no room in our program for half-measures and old ideas.

Understanding helps us cope with both the problems we face and our success in dealing with them. We will neither have doubts about the fact that our program works if we work it, nor will we be stubbornly insistent that we have all the answers.

In my Second Step, when I came to believe that a Power greater than myself could restore me to sanity, I began to understand my problems and what I must do to find solutions.

Admission

There are defeats more triumphant than victories.

—Michel de Montaigne

When we were using, did we ever admit anything without leaving ourselves a way out? Did we once unconditionally surrender and admit we were absolutely licked? How many times did we reach the end of the road and pretend it really wasn't? Why did it seem that enough was never enough for us? If there was any more misery or agony to be squeezed out of our lives, we seemed compelled to do so. What was it that held us back from a firm and final admission of our powerlessness over our addiction?

It was when we were flat on our backs with the heel of life pressed down on our throats that we heard ourselves moan to God, "this is, indeed, *the bottom*." It was then and only then that we made our First Step admission, a no-holds-barred surrender that the time had finally come to give it all up.

Admitting I was powerless seemed like the worst possible defeat. But I have come to realize it was the beginning of the greatest victory.

Unity

All your strength is in your union.
All your danger is in discord.
—Henry Wadsworth Longfellow

History is full of examples of how important unity in purpose and execution is in any act. Joining forces can create the triumph of good and the defeat of evil. "United we stand, divided we fall" has been a battle cry voiced by men and women from all nations and levels of society when they unite for a common cause.

Those in the program know from the very beginning of their recovery that building control over their addiction can never happen without the aid of others who have the same problems.

Early in our program of growth, we were told about our First Tradition, that our common welfare always comes first. Unless we recognize the fact that we need the help of other members, and are willing to go to any lengths to achieve success, we are headed for failure.

"One for all, and all for one" applies to my recovery. I can't do it alone.

Act Medium

Sign at a Twelve Step meeting: Nobody act big; nobody act small; everybody act medium.

—Anonymous

When we live medium, do we necessarily deny our greatness and our potential? The answer is no. When we live according to the slogan, "Nobody act big, nobody act small, everybody act medium," we acknowledge that everybody has greatness, and our greatness is not superior to anyone else's. This is hard for us because we are used to feeling special, sometimes low, sometimes high, but always special. Self-centeredness has caused us to want to be higher or lower than others. The fellowship and our Traditions teach us to rise side by side.

At our meetings we are careful to distinguish between our opinions and our experiences. It isn't as important to us that anyone listen to what we have to say as it is important that we freely share with the *hope* that it might be helpful to someone.

My ego fits itself to my heart and soul.
If my heart and soul are in line with my
Higher Power, my ego is in line.

• SEPTEMBER 6 •

Integrity

Tell me to live by yes and no: yes to everything good, no to everything bad.

—*William James*

When we were practicing our addictions, we lost track of what was right and wrong, honest or dishonest. Pride was defended. Anger was justified. Lust was accepted. Gluttony was encouraged. Envy was normal. Greed was there to be satisfied. Laziness was a way of life.

In recovery, regaining our integrity is difficult and confusing. Learning to be honest is hard when we've lost track of our souls. Working the Steps puts us in touch with our Higher Power, who is guiding us back to truth.

We finally come to recognize and rediscover the integrity in ourselves by simply knowing that what is *right* is what we feel *good* about and what is *wrong* is what we feel *bad* about.

I examine every thought and action to make sure it's right or wrong for me. If I don't feel good about it, I correct it as soon as it becomes clear to me that I've made a mistake. Learning to trust my thoughts and feelings again takes time and patience.

• SEPTEMBER 7 •

Rainy Days

Vexed sailors curse the rain, for which
poor shepherds prayed in vain.
—Edmund Waller

We lived our lives like a horse wearing blinders. We had tunnel vision and viewed the things around us with short-sightedness. Our attitudes were based on very few alternatives. We believed we could change things we couldn't.

What if the day turns out to be rainy? We can't call room service and order up a different kind of day! We either adjust our attitude to a rainy day or we elect to pout and sulk because it is raining.

The problem with many of us is that we have limited our outlook to just a few options. When we wake up to a rainy day and we check our "glad bag," we can't find our rainy-day joy-filled attitudes, because we have never cultivated an attitude of joy during bad weather. Sometimes we only have a sunny-day attitude in our glad bag and that does not fit a rainy day.

Loving and accepting myself requires that I learn to be good to myself each day. I can only work on what my attitude toward that day will be, whether it brings rain or shine.

• SEPTEMBER 8 •

Choices

Good thoughts bear good fruit, bad thoughts bear bad fruit—and man is his own gardener.
—John Leonard

Evil thoughts and destructive attitudes are not forced on us by fate. They are choices we make as we act and react to events in our lives.

Before the program, when negative things happened, our first reaction was to choose to react negatively: "Life's not fair. Why did that have to happen to me? I hate them for doing that. I'm going to get even if it's the last thing I do." It is easy to react positively when good things happen. But we have often chosen to react negatively to even good events.

Good can be found in even the worst situations if we look for it. Bankruptcy can provide a fresh start. Defeat can allow rebuilding in a new and better way. Evil teaches us what is good. Death brings new life. Admitting our powerlessness finally gave us the freedom to make choices.

By choosing good thoughts and attitudes, the garden of my soul will thrive. By choosing bad ones, it will shrivel and die.

Serenity

Serenity = Reality = Inner peace and strength
—*Anonymous*

Most of us chased an elusive thing called serenity for years. We thought our journeys outside reality brought us peace and serenity. When we returned to reality we found harshness and pain that caused us to run back to using. So it went, day after day, week after week, month after month, year after year. Run, escape, pain; run, escape, pain.

Then something happened. Our addiction wouldn't let us escape any more. We no longer found what we were seeking. We tried using more heavily. Finally, all that was left of our lives was the pain.

The fellowship shows us that reality is not a problem. Trying to escape reality is a problem. When we continue to turn our wills and lives over to a Higher Power, the serenity that results creates a reality of inner peace and strength.

I trust and believe that the changes
I am going through in my recovery
are necessary and good for me.

Opinions

Look for similarities rather than differences.
—Anonymous

By relating our experiences rather than our opinions, we allow the listener to form their own ideas, rather than be placed in a position of having either to agree or disagree with us.

For instance, if we express an opinion that "they *should* be honest," the listener may be put off.

However, if we tell an experience similar to their problem where honesty worked best for us, we aren't obligating the listener to solve their difficulty the same way. They're not forced into accepting or rejecting an opinion. They're still free to choose to solve their problem whatever way they see fit, and to profit from whatever experience results.

Opinions force me to take sides and "should" on myself and others. By sharing experiences instead of opinions, I am free to grow and to allow others to grow.

Reflection

Those who ask receive. Those who seek will find.
And to those who knock, the door will be opened.
—*Matthew 7:7–8*

Prayer is seeking answers and direction in life. Meditation is listening for answers from a Higher Power and developing the faith within us to accept those answers. Reflection is the study of ways to change the answers we get from prayer and meditation into *action*.

Reflection is the study of the meaning and uses of the Twelve Steps. It is not snap judgment. It requires consideration of the pros and cons of our possible choices and determination of what directions we will take to give us the best results.

The progress of spirituality from prayer to meditation to reflection is active, not passive. It is taking part in the joy of putting the results of prayer and meditation into action.

I have learned through times of quiet reflection to work into my life the answers my Higher Power has given me as a result of my prayer and meditation.

Anger

Anger is but one letter away from danger.
—Anonymous

Many of us once nursed long-standing resentments. Every time we thought about them, we got angry. What makes anger so dangerous is that it burns without consuming. It feeds on itself until it overwhelms all other emotions. Anger is poison.

When anger takes over, it acts with uncontrollable rage. We say things, feel things, and do things way out of line. Anger is emotional drunkenness. It leads to resentments, and it is a dangerous setup for a relapse.

Because we are in recovery doesn't mean we won't get angry, but the Steps give us a process of working through anger. We learn that what usually fuels anger is fear and guilt. When we deal with fear and guilt, we can dissolve anger. The remedy for fear is faith, for faith means courage.

When I replace my anger with faith, the fear and guilt that cause the anger are worked through, and the anger is reduced.

Pushing Buttons

Our family, parents, and loved ones can "push our buttons." That's because they installed them.

—*Anonymous*

Many of us grew up shame-based, and it has continued into our later lives. Addiction and shame go together. We were told we could do better in school. We were told we weren't living up to our potential. We learned there was *something* wrong with us. We *should* do better. Guilt is when we make a mistake; shame is when we *are* a mistake.

Our recovery allows us to identify and work out of our shame-based past. We can't force the people in our lives who push our buttons to change. We *can* change our attitudes and the way we react to button-pushers and the old unmanageable tapes in our heads. Not being perfect no longer means not being worthwhile.

Today I am learning not to let the button-pushers affect my outlook. My sponsor and friends are always there to make sure my button-pushers have much less power over me.

New Friends

Our friends are people who know
all about us and still like us.
—Anonymous

Because we are people who need people in order to maintain a happy recovery, we know that making friends can be one of our most important activities. We have overcome our "terminal uniqueness," isolation, and feelings of "being alone in a crowd." Sharing with friends in recovery is vital to our program.

We are told we can be an example of how our program works. When we make new friends in recovery, sharing our experiences and learning from theirs, we carry the message. To be a loner is to deny this to others. As recovering people, we need others in order to survive. Again we are reminded that no one can do it for us, but we can't do it alone.

By sharing with friends and making new ones,
I've overcome my "terminal uniqueness."
I carry the message and work my program.

• SEPTEMBER 15 •

Shortcomings

The unexamined life is not worth living.
—Socrates

None of us who strive for serenity will ever be tempted to say that we are leading a life that has gone unexamined. Our program places great emphasis on the Steps concerned with taking inventory of our lives and making definite moves to rid ourselves of shortcomings we find are slowing our progress. These Steps continue to stress a spiritual progress that can be maintained if we expect to cope with our problems.

We in recovery know that the inventory of defects of character needs to be fearless and thorough. Subsequent Steps involve us in admitting our wrongs to a Higher Power and humbly seeking God's help in relieving our lives of those handicaps. We continue to look at our behavior and make daily assessments of how we are living and handling our problems.

I am getting to know myself through my inventory taking. By examining and working to remove my shortcomings and character defects, my life has become worthwhile.

Solution

Be part of the solution, not the problem.
—*Anonymous*

When we were practicing our addiction, we traveled alone. We created short-term friendships with fellow users. These dissolved when the "party was over." Our addiction demanded from us absolute obedience. There could be no intimate friendships. No relationship was more important than the addiction. Anyone that moved in too close was beaten away by the disease. We were solitary, held hostage in our own prison.

The fellowship has broken the grip of this isolation. The miracle of recovery is that of men and women sharing their experience, strength, and hope with each other. We are together; we share with each other what we know, what we experience; we rely on each other. The fellowship is a circle of spiritual vitality that energizes anyone who decides to join hands.

Alone I am the problem. Together with others, I am part of the solution.

Sick and Tired

Sick and tired of being sick and tired.

—Anonymous

What a joy for us in recovery to discover mornings without a bleary-eyed hangover, a drugged-out case of nerves, or a bloated stomach. What a joy to taste food, smell flowers, sit without sweating, or go to sleep without passing out. What a joy to get into a car without fear of a DWI, without having to lie about where we were the night before. What a joy to stop swinging from pillar to post with every would-be lover, or finding ourselves a doormat for every Tom, Dick, or Mary.

We can wake up in the middle of the night without shaking with fear. We find that our Higher Power is doing for us what we can't do for ourselves. We have given up being "manipulators and operators" to become "true cooperators." We have hope for a better tomorrow.

The sick and tired existence of being sick and tired has finally come to an end.

Guilt

Try to replace guilt with gratitude.
—Anonymous

We could do very little in our lives while our disease ran unchecked. We hurt ourselves more than anyone. We did things we did not mean to do. We put off doing things we were going to do. We offended people we did not mean to offend. We were used to carrying such guilt and regret that it is a wonder more of us didn't seek recovery sooner.

In recovery, we learn how to free ourselves from old guilt. We learn how to make apologies, repay debts, and clean up mistakes through our Steps. We receive an unconditional forgiveness for our past life. We are not unworthy. What we are left with when the guilt is removed is gratitude. We become grateful for a chance to live a good life. We learn we do not have to live with new guilt because we do not have to do things for which we will feel guilty.

In the past, I did the best I could. Now I can do better. I would rather be standing on a mountain top with my arms extended in gratitude than in a hole holding a bucket of guilt.

• SEPTEMBER 19 •

Learn to Ask

I never learned anything talking. I only learn things when I ask questions.

—Lou Holtz

The low self-esteem we had when we began the program often prevented us from asking questions. It is natural for a newcomer to feel they are not worth the time required of a long-timer to give the advice needed. Many of us were afraid that those with solid recovery would be impatient with beginners.

The exact opposite was true. We realized that the experienced men and women in our program were able, willing, and eager to give us the benefits of what they had learned. Our questions reminded them how far they had come, and they were grateful for the reminder.

It was only after a time on the program that we came to believe wholeheartedly in the advice that "you have to give it away to keep it." By asking questions, we allow others to keep it by giving away their answers.

It is part of my recovery to admit how much I don't know. Wisdom began when I started asking questions.

Changes

Change your thoughts, and you change your world.
— Norman Vincent Peale

We learn from the program that all of our lives are made up of changes. Life for us can be like the seasons of the year. The uncomfortable blizzards of winter will pass. Spring brings flowers. Chattering birds fill the air with song where once there was wind, snow, and ice.

We know summer will follow spring. We learn to take the bad with the good. Hardships can make us stronger. Suffering cannot last forever. The key is to see life with optimism. We know that the changing of the seasons is like the changes in our lives.

When we use the Serenity Prayer, we may occasionally lose sight of its meaning. We need to concentrate on the differences between what we *can* change and what we *can't*.

I trust and believe that the changes in my recovery life are like the changing of the seasons. They are necessary and good for me.

Willingness

Willingness is the key.
—Anonymous

One by one, our disease consumed the many possibilities that filled life. Our addiction ate careers, marriages, homes. We always wanted one more chance, one more opportunity to make it on our own. The disease told us that we were strong enough, smart enough, ready enough to do anything we wanted. It's the only disease that tells us we don't have it.

There is only one kind of willingness that will work in the face of this disease of denial: the willingness to take certain Steps and not pick up the first drink or do the first drug; the willingness to admit that the disease had an uncontrollable power over us and that our lives were unmanageable. We were told that if we are honest, we had a chance. We needed to be ready to go to any lengths to put an end to our disease. This was necessary because we lived with a disease that would go to any lengths to kill us.

When I let go of my ego's destructive self-will,
I began to understand that my growth and
happiness are based on my willingness
to change for the better.

Self-Esteem

Nobody holds a good opinion of a man who has a low opinion of himself.

—*Anthony Trollope*

We often hear, "It takes what it takes." Recovery works for those who not only want it badly enough, but also know the program will improve their self-esteem if they work at it. We also know that we cannot succeed unless we follow the Steps of the program and continue to work with others in every way.

To succeed, we have to stop thinking we are *less* than other people. We tell ourselves we are not unworthy, inadequate, or unable to cope fully with life's problems. We begin to see the glass as half-full, instead of half-empty. We have to get rid of feelings of inability before we can make progress. If we change our thoughts, we change ourselves.

By holding a positive attitude based on an honest and realistic self-knowledge of myself, I will continue to build my self-esteem and have the esteem of others.

Pass It On

It is well to give when asked, but it is better to give unasked, through understanding.
— Kahlil Gibran

Each of us is equally responsible for the future well-being of our fellowship. Each of us, having had a spiritual awakening as a result of these Steps, is called on to carry the message to others and to continue practicing these principles in all our affairs.

The key to our ever-present renewal as a fellowship is the fact that we can't stay recovered unless we share our recovery. It is always in our self-interest to pass it on. The sharing we do in our meetings acts like a breeder reactor for recovery.

When we're asked to share, we can "Pass it on." But we can also "Pass it on" by simply understanding even when not asked. In our first meeting, we knew that these people understood what we were going through even without their sharing. That feeling kept us coming back. We knew we were home.

The program has taught me that
the price for serenity and sanity is
self-sacrifice. I will pass it on.

No Sainthood

Life leads never to perfection
but always toward it.
—James Lane Allen

Our friends in the program repeatedly pound into our heads: "We are not saints." The improvement we make in recovery could easily lead us to believe that we may be approaching sainthood. That idea doesn't last past one honest inventory. Old-timers remind us "Don't try to be a saint by Thursday."

If we believe we are superior because of our success in recovery, we will find ourselves impossible to live with. We seek spiritual progress rather than spiritual perfection. Perfection is impossible for humans to achieve. Our limitations, as well as our potentials, add to our spiritual growth.

Those who have all the answers for themselves and others, and reject suggestions or advice are probably headed toward relapse.

One of the best pieces of advice for improving
myself and my attitude is "Easy does it."
There really isn't anything beyond
the very best I can do.

Anonymity

Respect the anonymity of others.
—Anonymous

The spiritual foundation of our program is anonymity. In the fellowship we are not Dan the Mechanic, Mary the New Mother, or Linda the Office Manager. We are just Dan, Mary, and Linda. Each one of has paid a great price to earn our seat around the tables. There is nothing that has cost us so much as our membership in the fellowship. The miracle of recovery is what occurs within a meeting when we listen to honest stories of changed lives.

We remember that what makes it work is the common bond of our addiction. We are to take what we need and leave all that we hear and see at that meeting. When we respect the anonymity of others, we respect our own.

The people who share with me do so to support their own recovery, not to give me information about themselves. When I protect the anonymity of the fellowship, I protect my own recovery.

Seeking Balance

Success is living a life that makes a difference. The question to ask is whether or not the world is a better place because of your efforts.

—*Anonymous*

Most of our errors are small, but they can be very painful. They range from carelessness to excessiveness. The way to a comfortable existence is a balance between overdoing everything and being complacent. Finding a halfway point is necessary. Otherwise, we will bounce from self-pity to arrogance.

We understand that growth stops if we cannot make up our minds between being grandiose and sitting on the pity pot. We can be troubled by an excess of love as easily as being filled with hatred. All too often, we may say with regret, "I'm killing them with kindness." Inability to find balance in what life offers us may end in our being hurt or very disappointed. When we think problems and their solutions are black or white, either-or, and this or that, we make impulsive choices between only one or two alternatives. This gets us stuck.

Unless I practice balance, I will find myself in an emotional tug-of-war between extremes.

Spot Checks

I'm slipping when I shrink from self-examination.

—Anonymous

Working our program smooths our path to a new way of life. We must keep following the simple instructions outlined in the Steps. One of these is to continue to take a personal inventory and whenever we are wrong, promptly admit it.

When we do this Step each day, molehills don't become mountains. If we don't continue with spot-check inventories, we allow garbage to build up once again in our lives. We've seen that a buildup of resentment and guilt can lead to trouble. Stinking thinking thrives on this garbage. If we shrink from self-examination, fear creeps back into our lives. Fear pushes out faith. Without faith we lose our recovery.

My daily spot-check inventory is one of the important things that keeps my program working.

Experience

Trust one who has gone through it.
—Virgil

Non-members can be experienced and helpful in treating addictions and helping us in recovery, but it is very important for us to learn from others in the program.

There is no way to fool another addict. Trust is born when newcomers find they are being helped by another person who has gone through what they are going through. Hope is born when they see that member living a sane and manageable life.

Through the fellowship, we are not alone when we face the problems of recovery. Those who have been in the program for years and who are enjoying quality sobriety are always close with advice and aid. We trust them because we know that they know. Sometimes we also need to be with our fellow travelers just so we can laugh, play, and be with people.

If they can do it, so can I. I am wise to hang around those who know from experience.

Depressions

Don't look down unless you plan on staying there.

—Anonymous

Depressions and setbacks are a part of life for us even when we are solidly active in our program. We were told early that an addict's highs are always higher than the ordinary and their lows lower. When things begin going wrong (and the law of averages predicts that things will), we can feel depressed even when we compare these lows with the good feelings we experience when we grow spiritually.

At times of depression, we can find relief and change our attitude by entering into the caring and sharing of our program. It is certain that we can never overcome our down times alone and without help. We always remind ourselves that depressions will not fade unless we have the help of others, sometimes professional help. Many are also helped with the blues when they get out of themselves and help others.

To handle my depressions and low points, I need the help of my friends in the program. I can't do it alone.

Growth

Let each become all that he was created capable of being . . . expand, if possible, to his full growth.

— Thomas Carlyle

Growth is change. It is a necessity in recovery. As our attitudes, actions, and thinking grow, we are aware of the miracle of change in our lives. Our growth becomes evidence of an exciting life. Our growth in character is a result of how well we learn, with gratitude and humility, from experience.

Spiritual, emotional, and physical growth becomes apparent when time and experience cause us to be gentle with ourselves. This happens when we use realistic self-criticism as we review our behavior. Long-timers tell us that "you've got to grow or you've got to go." And we don't ever want to go back to what we were.

Growth is change. When I am willing to grow spiritually, emotionally, physically, and mentally, I change for the better.

OCTOBER

• OCTOBER 1 •

Amends

The first step in overcoming
mistakes is to admit them.
—Anonymous

Amends for us are basically honest apologies of the deepest and most sincere kind. We ask not only forgiveness from others but from ourselves as well. As we forgive, we grow spiritually. We are aware of unkindnesses we performed and the unhappiness we heaped not only on those we thought we disliked but on many whom we loved. We realize the potential for hurting others contained in our acts and words.

Sending a note or making a phone call may not be enough. We are most effective making an amend directly if at all possible. We'll find most people are very open to talking about amends and are glad to work on finding a way to put the past to rest. This keeps us aware of being kind to others.

When I make sincere and honest apology
for a wrong I've done, I feel better for
having done the right thing.

Pink Clouds

Be not afraid of life. Believe that life is worth living, and your belief will create the fact.
—William James

Nearly all of us refer at some time to being on a "honeymoon of recovery." Whether we call it a "honeymoon" or "being on a pink cloud," the experience is the same. The recovery honeymoon is a natural state of well-being after we get the monkey off our backs.

The sensation of living on a pink cloud never has to leave us, but we can only keep it by moving into positive action and working our program. This is a time of being physically, emotionally, and spiritually at peace with society and ourselves. It has been described as a time of joy that makes us feel we are climbing out of darkness into light. Like other miracles of recovery, pink clouds are reality, not fantasy.

I can keep living on my "pink cloud" of recovery if I keep working at it and practicing gratitude and humility.

Slogans

Live easy but think first.
—Anonymous

"Live and let live," "Easy does it," "But for the grace of God," "Think, think, think," and "First things first" are the five slogans we most often hear and see on the walls of our meeting rooms. The first word of each of these five slogans also creates a popular slogan: "Live easy but think first."

Many newcomers hear that we begin recovery on the slogans and stay in recovery on the Twelve Steps. The slogans were developed for use in recovery from the experience of many others. They at first appear to us as too simple (and sometimes too corny) for our use. The slogans are anything but corny. We need to check if we are using them in our daily lives.

The slogans helped me when I first came in. I continue to use them to keep me on the program, but I also remember not to be a "slogan slinger" and ram them down everyone's throat.

Forgiveness

To err is human, to forgive divine.
—Alexander Pope

True healing requires that we give back freely what we received freely. We have been accepted by our Higher Power and forgiven our mistakes. We must pass on that forgiveness. We have to learn to accept the fact that we sometimes hurt others in ways of which we are not aware. If a person comes to us and asks for forgiveness, it is important for our own well-being that we pass it on.

It does us no good to hang on to resentments and bitterness for another person. This is an extremely serious matter. Our recovery can be in danger if we withhold our forgiveness. It is equally true that there is nothing we have done for which we cannot be forgiven. God's love for us is unlimited. We need only ask. We always have an opportunity for a second start.

I forgive as I am forgiven. I have learned in recovery to accept being human and not perfect. What I am is different from what I used to think I should or ought to be.

Own Worst Enemy

We have met the enemy, and he is us.
—Walt Kelly

We can quit being our own worst enemy by developing the willingness to be good to ourselves. When we feel uptight, we all tend to treat ourselves unkindly. We can begin to like ourselves if we keep thinking about how far we've come in our recovery. We have figuratively gone all the way to hell and made a U-turn.

We can't forgive others their mistakes and not forgive ourselves as well. If we consider ourselves our own worst enemy, we aren't listening to our friends in the program or our Higher Power. They tell us to be kind, to ourselves and others.

Acceptance is knowing we are good and whole despite our limitations and defects. As long as we strive to improve, we are free to take joy in who we are now.

When I feel like my own worst enemy,
I'm in danger of hating myself. Perfection
isn't possible, but progress is.

• OCTOBER 6 •

Character Defects

The only truths we can point to are the ever-changing truths of our own experience.

—*Peter Weiss*

We once wore our character defects like badges of honor. We were comfortable with them. They seemed natural and normal to us. We believed in our defects. We believed we needed them.

The ego of which we were so proud has had to be deflated. When God becomes our primary focus, our character traits are shown to us in a new light. We are able to ask for help from our Higher Power to get rid of the parts of our character that hurt us.

We know that if we are not ready and willing for the help of our Higher Power and our friends, we will not get rid of our character defects.

I must be willing to see myself in a new way and accept myself as I am. That way I can start changing my defects that hurt me and my recovery.

• OCTOBER 7 •

Making Progress

Bring the body, the mind will follow.
—Anonymous

Progress is a word of action, but for us it must never be hurried. We are told, "the idea is to make improvement, not finish first at a destination." There's no need to rush. We can take time to think about the direction we're going. Sometimes spiritual progress may seem slow to us, but if we honestly work the program, that progress is sure.

We can also take the time to examine the progress we have made. When we realize how far we have come, it makes it possible for us to continue. Practicing the Eleventh Step will help us slow down and calm our urgent need to always be rushing around.

I must never stand still. Even when I stop and look at my progress, that is an action that gives me the courage to continue.

• OCTOBER 8 •

Limitations

The four As: Acceptance, Awareness, Action, Attitude

—Anonymous

It is as important for us to live within our limitations as it is to live up to our capabilities. Step One tells us that we do not have a limit but that we are limited. We admit this when we begin our growth in the Twelve Steps. The action Step, the final one, reminds us that we can only try to practice the principles of our program in all our affairs.

And, of course, we must accept the truth that we seek spiritual progress not spiritual perfection. In admitting limitations we are reminding ourselves that we are only human. When we keep ourselves from trying to play God, we admit our imperfections. We seek our Higher Power's help in lessening our limitations when we take inventories and remember the four As: Acceptance, Awareness, Action, and Attitude.

My program is based on my learning to live with my limitations. I will also remember that I need to live up to my capabilities.

• OCTOBER 9 •

Changing

All changes, even the most longed for, have [some sadness]; for what we leave behind us is a part of ourselves; we must die to one life before we can enter into another!

—*Anatole France*

Changing negative patterns of behavior has been difficult for most of us. The harder we tried to change ourselves, the less we seemed to succeed. We believed we wanted what was good for us, yet our actions proved otherwise. Our addiction showed us that willpower was more of a barrier to change than a help.

Before recovery, we used to read books written on how to become happy, quit bad habits, and improve the quality of our lives. We read the words, believed what they said, and continued to live as we always had.

Now we look to our recovery for an answer. We can let go of our old familiar ways that gave us the illusion of safety. We now see how they were self-defeating.

I have learned in recovery not to be stubborn or afraid of changing. I can live in the present and build a better future.

The Past

Let go and let God. What's turned over turns out.

—*Anonymous*

There is a bit of packrat in all of us. We've carried things around with us that should have been thrown away long ago. We have had bad experiences that we can recall in an instant. We play the scene back in our minds and bring up those old feelings, and suddenly we are back in time. We feel the anxiety, anger, and resentment of the moment.

We learn in recovery not to carry the effects of old feelings into our present reality. We ask our Higher Power for the willingness to let go and turn over those memories. All they do is cause us pain and remorse. Our willingness to venture beyond the past into the present is the key to the future.

I will learn what I can from my past. Then I turn it over and put it behind me in order to build my future. I trust my Higher Power to take over all the things I've tried to control.

Faith and Trust

Faith is not belief without proof,
but trust without reservation.
—Anonymous

We had only to meet the first person that greeted us in the first meeting we attended in our recovery to know that the program worked. Our faith in how it works is illustrated for us by the lives of millions of men and women who are recovering.

If we rely on miracles to develop a faith, our program can be an unlimited provider of them. The real issue for the person in recovery is one of trust, the day-in, day-out, come-what-may trust in a Higher Power. What was discovered by the early members of our fellowship has been rediscovered time and again in every meeting where members gather to share their recovery: that we can unreservedly trust in God to do for us what we cannot do for ourselves.

I have learned a new meaning to the word faith: *trust in a Higher Power, in the program, and in myself.*

Alternatives

A person is usually not attached to anything more than their own suffering.

—Anonymous

We all have a choice between widely separated alternatives. We can like ourselves or hate ourselves. We can lift ourselves up or put ourselves down. We can be for ourselves or against ourselves. Actions, attitudes, and thinking determine the direction of our choices. We can have more self-esteem and happiness, or we can be depressed and miserable. The negative approach always is the easiest.

It takes little effort to be a sufferer. It is said that some addicted people can never feel comfortable unless they are uncomfortable. Fortunately, we don't have to think unkindly of ourselves, even when we are remembering what kind of person we used to be. We have alternatives. It is wise to take them.

I am responsible for my recovery. I have alternatives and the choices are mine. With the help of my Higher Power, I will make the right ones.

Remember When

We can be positive that our active addiction was negative.

—*Anonymous*

The memory of our First Step is a memory we want to keep always fresh in our minds. The First Step asks us to "remember when."

We never leave our First Step. It is current history. It is now. We will hear in meetings someone tell a story of relapse. "After three months, I went out. . . . After six months . . . After one year . . ."

We never outgrow our First Step. In fact, we never have more than one day of abstinence. We all have one more relapse in us, but do we have one more recovery? We go to meetings first and foremost to remember who we are and what it used to be like. When we want to go to a meeting, we can walk; when we don't, we should run.

I will always "remember when."
When I forget about my First Step,
I am destined to repeat it again.

Letting Go

I can't handle it, God. You take over.

—Anonymous

The life we lived in the dark world of our disease was a terrifying one. It was as if we were perched on a tiny ledge thousands of feet up the side of a mountain. The drop was straight down. We never dared to look up or down because we so desperately feared falling. All we could do was feed our disease and tremble in fear. We were stuck. There was no room on our ledge for anyone else. We were all alone. Every day, little bits and pieces of our perch would fall off. All we could do was wait.

Finally, out of desperation, we looked up and saw thousands of people urging us to climb. They reached down and created a human chain for us to climb. All we had to do was let go of our perch and take the hands extended to us. We stood, looked up, let go, and took the hands. We were safe.

I'm not stuck any more. I've let go of my fear and accept help when I need it.

Attitudes

The great scorer . . . marks not that you won or lost, but how you played the game.
—Grantland Rice

When we are told that "some are sicker than others," we are reminded that we might also say, "some of us are more well than others." Both statements are correct. We remember that "we are not bad people trying to become good, but are sick individuals trying to get well, physically, mentally, and spiritually."

All of us who remain abstinent, grow, and make positive changes in recovery are winners. But there is no competition with others in the program. We all work together, as a team. Most of us do not consider those who relapse as losers. More aptly are they called "quitters." Each member plays the game by simple rules and to the best of an individual's ability.

There is no scoring, no giving of grades,
and no graduation in the school of recovery.
How I work the program is up to me and
determines the quality of my recovery.

Admitting Wrongs

A man should never be ashamed to own he has been in the wrong, which is but saying, in other words, that he is wiser today than he was yesterday.

—*Alexander Pope*

No one can grow spiritually until they have cleared their conscience and gained the respect and forgiveness of others by admitting their wrongs. Only by wiping the slate clean can we free ourselves of the constant painful reminders of acts and words that have left us with regrets, guilt, and shame. Of course, we can't be free of thoughts about the past until we have learned, through thorough inventories, the nature of our mistakes.

Our admission of wrongdoing may help others understand us better, but the person most benefited from the admission is us. The process of admitting wrongs assures us that we have accepted honesty as an asset we need in our new way of life.

The sooner I admit my mistakes,
the easier they are to correct. Let me
promptly admit it when I am wrong.

Action

Faith is spelled A-C-T-I-O-N.
—Anonymous

Again and again, we are told that our recovery program is, above all, one of action. We are constantly reminded that "nobody can do it for you." Yet the action in our program is not a singular effort. It involves every member.

In a boatload of people, one person paddling with a single oar will make little progress. Everyone must row if the whole boatload is to survive. Our program truly is a fellowship. We all work together toward our common goal, recovery. Each of us contributes to the progress of all.

During the times we were driven by our addictions and compulsions, we were often uneasy about our friendships. The new friendships we've found in recovery are some of the rewards of our present lifestyle.

I am learning that unless I take action to further my recovery, faith and growth are impossible. But I need my friendships also. In recovery, I don't "think less of myself, I think of myself less."

Grandiosity

There are none too dumb for the program,
but many are too smart.

—Anonymous

Most of us suffered from some degree of grandiosity. We had inflated egos, were self-centered, stubborn, impatient, headstrong, selfish, and pushy. We liked to think in terms of the big picture. We liked big deals and big plans. We carried around a feeling that we knew everything, that we were godlike.

If we don't reduce our grandiosity in recovery, we are looking for trouble. When we act like big shots, we only *submit* to the program, we don't *surrender*. We favor negative thinking, hold back from inventories and making amends, make little effort at finding a Higher Power, avoid prayer, neglect finding a sponsor, don't read, and are bored at most meetings.

Today I'll remember that when I am
a big shot and have grandiose thoughts,
I don't listen, share, or get involved.

• OCTOBER 19 •

Fault-Finding

I'm slipping when I begin taking another person's inventory, not mine.

—Anonymous

It seems so much easier to live someone else's life than it is to live our own. We can see someone else's faults much more clearly than our own. We can tell someone else how to correct a character defect, and not work on our own. It is easier to take someone else's inventory than it is to take our own. These are all clues to why we have had so much trouble in our lives.

These things are all danger signs. Our very best thinking got us into this fellowship. Most of us earned our seats around the table by totally mismanaging the affairs of our lives. We have enough on our plates trying to sort out the will of our Higher Power in our own lives. We have no business trying to run anyone else's.

If I persist in trying to live another person's life, I am likely to stop my spiritual progress. Let me remember to keep tabs on my own faults and let others take care of their own.

Positive Outlook

Flying is largely a matter of having the right outlook.

—E.B. White

We may not make it if we don't have the outlook that success is within our reach if we practice the principles of our program. Nobody believed that it would ever be possible for man to fly. Then the Wright brothers proved that it could be done. What was said to be impossible was there to be achieved.

Naturalists have proved for centuries that the bumblebee technically can't fly. But the bumblebee doesn't know that, so it continues to amaze them by flying.

A positive outlook is necessary if we are to make our program fly. When we lose that positive outlook, we lose hope and crash. Optimism means letting go of worry about the future. The future is in the hands of our Higher Power, and there's no better place for it to be.

With a positive outlook, I can accomplish success in my recovery program. Without it, I'm going nowhere.

Healthy Pride

The only person keeping us from having self-worth is ourselves.

—Anonymous

Having healthy pride in our accomplishments in recovery is fine as long as it is coupled with gratitude and humility. As long as we don't settle for an inferior quality of recovery and continue to strive for the best, that kind of pride will not cause harm.

However, pride out of control is dangerous. Too many are certain they "wrote the book." They take false pride in their accomplishments and feel they have nothing left to learn. They are eager to tell everyone how much they know. This is a sure way of closing a mind that desperately needs to be wide open. This kind of pride has turned into arrogance that causes many people to "turn off."

False pride and settling for inferiority will accomplish nothing. I no longer choose to have low self-worth.

Being Humble

Humility is not thinking less of yourself,
but thinking of yourself less.

—*Anonymous*

Humility was confusing to us when we were new to the program. Our first reaction was to think we were supposed to accept anything that came our way, however humiliating. But true humility doesn't mean a meek surrender to an ugly, destructive way of life. It means surrender to the will of our Higher Power. "Humility" and "humiliation" are entirely different things.

Being humble is *being teachable*. Humility opens us to growth in all other helpful ways of living a healthy and productive life. Through humility, we gain more faith, trust, hope, helpfulness, forgiveness, charity, and the ability to freely care and share.

The simple practice of gratitude, listening, and sharing help us cut through grandiosity and leads us toward growth in humility.

When I practice humility, I am growing
in strength and making spiritual progress.

• OCTOBER 23 •

Optimism

The program works if you want it to work.
—Anonymous

Rarely do climbers stare up to see how far away the top still is. Instead, when they rest, they look down toward the starting point of their journey. The view they see assures them that they have already come a long, long way.

Like the climbers, we need to keep our eyes on where we are and where we've been, not on where we're going. When we become discouraged with the progress of our recovery, we only need to look back over how far we have come. The rewarding "view" gives us courage to continue. Many of us recall times when we lived without hope and the sense of impending doom. Now we look forward to life with confidence.

Today I will remember to face my climb
with optimism. Even if my progress
sometimes seems slow to me, it's still
a long way from where I once was.

Honesty

Honesty is largely a matter of information,
of knowing that dishonesty is a mistake.
—Edgar Watson Howe

If honesty is the best policy, most of us were delinquent in following it before we found recovery. We were reluctant to tell the truth because we were afraid of the consequences. Our dishonesties led us away from our true selves. We felt we were living behind hundreds of masks. We tried to put the world together through our manipulations.

We were always whole and complete. It was our lying, dishonesty, and rationalizations that made us feel small. When we honestly look at our life now and account for our actions, we reclaim our identity. This is a wonderful experience. We can take pleasure in the unique person that we are, and continue to build a new life.

Honesty keeps me in the present reality
and opens the door to the future.
I never need to hide again.

• OCTOBER 25 •

Miracles

The age of miracles is forever here.
—Thomas Carlyle

Regardless of whatever addiction it was that sent us for help to the program, we all refer to the big and small miracles of recovery that we experience. The chains of our addiction were so strong that we considered ourselves helpless and hopeless. We know that only a miracle saved our lives. There seemed no way out for us until we began to share experiences, strengths, and hopes with others who were in recovery, who were once as sick and desperate as we were.

To live without our substance seemed impossible. Small wonder that we began to believe in personal miracles when we found abstinence. One of the miracles was being able to care and share with others. Another miracle made service easy and natural.

Every moment I don't use is a miracle. That I believe in a Higher Power is a miracle. That I have forgiven myself and love others is a miracle. The age of miracles begins with recovery.

• OCTOBER 26 •

Identification

Identify, don't compare.
—*Anonymous*

When we *identify* with another in recovery, we bond with that person, and in so doing, we pass on the message of recovery. When we *compare* our program with that of another, we break the bond and become separated by an act of our own ego. We can't grow when we compare.

The hope we all share in our fellowship is that we will come to experience an honest acceptance of what life has to offer. We will never receive a report card grading our progress or a diploma for working the Steps. Taking our inventory is not the same as keeping score. We do not compare our program with that of any other person. We only share our experiences to help another fellow traveler. We never try to put ourselves above anyone else through comparisons.

Identifying with my fellow travelers
helps us to help each other. Comparing
my progress with theirs turns recovery
into a competition nobody wins.

• OCTOBER 27 •

Patience

How poor are they that have no patience.
—William Shakespeare

Patience is important to our growth and peace of mind. Without patience, we would have difficulty holding down anxiety, anger, envy, and unreasonable pride. Patience has often prevented disaster threatened by a loose tongue or an impulsive fist. Patience has taught us to stay cheerful in hard times and to quickly forgive mistakes.

Faith, peace, love, and humility all "study" in the school of patience. We learn patience from nature's careful maturing of crops. Baby chicks are born from letting eggs hatch, not by quickly smashing the shell. We are reminded that time is a faithful servant.

When we set goals that we can reach and are patient with our progress, we save ourselves a lot of anxiety. Happiness is not having what we *want*, but wanting what we *have*.

I need to be patient, but I don't have to "grin and bear it." I can accept reality then take careful positive action.

Stinking Thinking

I affirm life; I challenge problems; I accept responsibility; I believe in God; I live today.
—Elizabeth Lamb

It's not good looks, a charming personality, or brain power that keeps us in recovery. It's our *attitude* that makes the difference. Our disease is characterized by the reality of relapse. Most relapses come from a *bad* attitude. In the fellowship, we call that "Stinking thinking." Attitudes lead us toward a healthy and happy recovery, or into relapse. It's our choice.

When our attitudes are bad, we "Talk the talk," but don't "Walk the walk." We tell people what they want to hear, but we really don't believe what we're saying. We act grandiose. We think we don't need to follow all the principles and disciplines of the program. Stinking thinkers keep their minds closed. They are defensive and blame others for their problems. Having a bad attitude doesn't always lead to relapse, but it's like putting one foot out the door.

When my thinking starts to stink, I check my commitment to my recovery and remember I am responsible for the attitudes I choose.

A Swelled Head

The true snob never rests; there is always a higher goal to attain, and there are, by the same token, always more and more people to look down upon.

—*Russell Lynes*

Recovery feels good! It feels good to get a good night's sleep, eat right, have friends, and be more at peace. After a while on the program our foggy minds cleared up. We could actually read and remember what we read. Our emotions calmed down. We felt proud of our progress.

At moments like these we must remember by whose Power we achieve such joy. It is not our own. If we let ourselves think we did it all on our own, pride swells our head and stops our growth. We can become cocky, thinking we've got it made, and drift back to slippery people and places.

A swelled head has no place in my program. I must keep in mind that I didn't get this far to rest and stop growing.

Self-Confidence

Alas, the fearful disbelief is disbelief in yourself.
—Thomas Carlyle

Self-confidence is an important lesson we learn in our recovery. Most of us start our program with little confidence in ourselves. As we work the Steps, we begin to be confident that we can be whatever we choose to be, if we want success enough and if we keep on growing.

When we have no faith in ourselves, we have little chance of staying abstinent. Even the miracles of recovery cannot accomplish a better way of living if we don't believe they can. The more we share with fellow members, the greater will be our self-confidence that success is possible.

In order to have and maintain self-confidence, and feel good mentally and physically, we need to keep our heads screwed on straight with clear and rational thinking.

I can be whoever I make myself believe I can.

Respect

FAITH is a lighted doorway, but TRUST is the dark hallway that says, "Do I dare walk this way, not knowing where it will lead?"

—Anonymous

When we have faith in others we are giving them a great gift. We are giving them respect. By the time we found our way into recovery, most of us had lost respect for ourselves and others. We had lost faith in our own judgment. We couldn't tell a truth from a lie.

When we began to regain our faith in ourselves, we weren't sure if it was right to do so or not. When we shared with others as honestly as we could, we found that they trusted us to tell the truth. And we had the unfamiliar sensation that they respected our honesty and us.

We found that sharing honestly created trust in the integrity of others. And they responded the same way to us. Mutual trust then blossomed through faith.

When I share honestly with others in the program, I am building faith, respect, and trust between us.

• NOVEMBER 1 •

Keep Coming Back

Keep coming back; it works if you work it.
—Anonymous

Our memories can be very short. Staying close to the program and attending meetings is important in keeping our memories current. Addictions have a way of patiently waiting for us to stop working our program. Addictions know that when we stop working, it is only a matter of time before they take over again.

There will never be a graduation from meetings, and we will never have more than this day to judge our progress. We succeed or fail one day at a time, one meeting at a time.

Many of us can say with some certainty that we do not have another recovery in us. If we relapse, we may never come back. There is no certainty in recovery; there is no perfection; there is only progress. We attend meetings to make that progress.

I have to keep coming back to stay in recovery. My recovery will keep working for me if I continue to work it.

Cheerfulness

Cheerfulness keeps up a kind of daylight in the mind and fills it with a steady and perpetual serenity.

—Joseph Addison

All spiritual growth points us toward serenity. When we find it, we also find a cheerful attitude. When we feel at peace with the world we "put on a happy face." In our program, we refer to that state as being "happy, joyous, and free."

Cheerfulness is a personal choice. It begins with our acceptance of reality as we continue to grow spiritually. When we give our cheerfulness to others, we are also keeping for ourselves the peace that emotional growth brings us.

Cheerfulness is a big part of a positive attitude. Without it, we wouldn't be able to accept the things we need to accept. Cheerfulness can't exist without freedom.

Peace of mind and serenity are never forced on me. I must have an open heart and open mind to receive it.

Fixing Others

Don't fix; be supportive.
—Anonymous

If it was within our capacity to fix people's lives, we would have done so a long time ago with all our friends and relatives. We finally realized in our First Step how hopelessly mismatched we were for the job of fixing ourselves and the whole world. Most of us struggled for years to fix our own lives, but we couldn't. It was not until we admitted we were licked that we finally got the help we needed. By working the other eleven Steps, we came to believe that a Power greater than us could fix what we couldn't.

Our role in life changes as a result of the Steps. We watch the way God might be moving in the life of a friend or loved one, and we aim to support God's handiwork. We watch the ways our sponsor offers support, always encouraging us to accept situations we cannot change, or getting back to change situations we can.

When I try to fix others, it doesn't work very well. All I can really do is be supportive in their efforts and focus on fixing myself.

• NOVEMBER 4 •

Security

I'm gonna stand my ground, won't be turned around, and I'll keep this world from draggin' me down. Gonna stand my ground, and I won't back down.

— *Tom Petty*

Security is the result of a dedicated effort toward a goal. We feel secure in our fellowship, some more, some less. Security comes from the safety and confidence we get from building on the working principles of our program of spiritual growth.

We know that our progress can never be taken away from us by force or underhanded dealings of others. Our belief in the security of the program defies those who try to betray our trust or draw us back into addiction. Security is the knowledge that it is possible for the most hopeless and helpless victims of any addiction to find recovery. Security is also a shield against our own acts of carelessness or feelings of overconfidence.

I have come to feel secure in the program and my recovery. I won't let others or myself bring me down.

Crises

A problem shared is a problem halved.
—Anonymous

Working the Steps strengthens us to meet crises head on. Above all, the Steps show us that we never need to fear problems like we did in the old days. We learn to face crises with confidence and a faith in our ability to cope. When a crisis brings us up against a problem that is a complete surprise, we meet it with an effort to do the best we can. We ask the help of others and our Higher Power.

Crises come in all sizes. They can be minor annoyances or earthshaking adventures, but we know that we must always confront a crisis as soon as it develops. Recovery doesn't promise us a life without crises, but a better way in dealing with them. Helping others in trouble and giving away the knowledge we have been given by coping with crises helps us grow spiritually.

Today I'll remember to face crises
when they happen, and cope with them.
I will ask for help when I need it.

Broken Hearts

Time wasted in getting even can never be used in getting ahead.

—Anonymous

Many of us, during the course of our lives, experience a number of broken relationships. Some of them are very painful and stay with us for years. We often feel we have been harmed and hold onto deep resentments about the rejection. After many days, months, sometimes years, we bury our broken heart and carry on with our lives.

Step Eight asks us to take another look at these relationships. We must dig up our broken heart and assume our responsibility for our part in the break. We come to discover that, whether we like it or not, we all have a part in the breakdown of a relationship. The way to help us heal a broken relationship is to make amends. As hard as it may be for us, we must make every effort except where we may harm someone. We must be honest, even if it means the amends are not returned.

Today I'll remember that relationships always have two sides. I will take responsibility for my part in broken ones, and make amends where I can to the best of my ability.

Self-Approval

We can gain other people's approval if we do right and try hard but our own approval is worth a hundred times more.

—Mark Twain

It is a plus factor in character growth if others like us, especially if they believe we are worth knowing. But unless *we* like who we really are, what we are doing, and what we want to make of ourselves by our own efforts, we are in danger of making little progress in building our self-esteem.

We learn to be gentle with ourselves. We learn that not only do we forgive others but also we forgive ourselves. We develop an honest pride in how we have grown in our recovery program. We have learned in our program that people-pleasing is a dead end. Those who, at times, feel that they are not really changing, should look in mirrors.

Learning to like myself is one of the most valuable lessons the program teaches me. My life is mine and not based on other people's approval.

Beginnings

A journey of a thousand miles
must begin with a single step.
—Lao Tzu

No effort on our part was too small when we decided that we truly *wanted* the new life offered to us by the program. Great rivers begin with tiny springs. The healthful flow of our recovery began when we took our First Step. We began to take action and were responsible for our progress.

We learn that we can never stand with raised arms, calling out, "shower me with your gifts." When we read the promises of our program, we are reminded that they will materialize *if we work for them.* Not a single inch of progress could begin until the First Step of surrender and acceptance was taken.

My recovery journey began with my First Step.
Each Step after that has taken me further on
my path of spiritual progress. I remind myself
that "recovery is discovery."

Expectations

For people who live on expectations, to face up to their realization is something of an ordeal.

—Elizabeth Bowen

We used to undermine our happiness with unrealistic expectations. We said we wanted to be happy, but our actions told a different story. We held onto resentments and grudges, because we expected life to be fair. We expected those around us to understand our needs with no effort on our part. We expected to be given all the good things in life simply because we thought we deserved to have them handed to us.

Our program teaches us to let go of expectations. We learn to face reality. We realize that life is not handed to us on a silver platter. We come to appreciate reality. We need to make fewer unrealistic demands on ourselves, others, and life in general.

When I live on expectations, I am not living in the real world. I need to tone down my demands and appreciate the life I am living right now.

Miracles

The age of miracles is forever here.
— Thomas Carlyle

So many wonderful, unexpected things happen to us in recovery. We are convinced early in the program that miracles can happen to all who work toward spiritual progress. The fact that we found our way to the program is itself a miracle. That we have learned how to stay abstinent is another. That we are living a new and better life is still another.

With the help of our friends, our program, and our Higher Power, we experience miracles of discovery and growth all the time. As long as we face each day with honesty and gratitude, those miracles will continue to be ours.

It is said that the greatest miracle would be to return from the dead. Before recovery began, we were among the living dead. Today we are all miracles.

Today and every day, I will remember to thank my Higher Power for the miracles I've found in recovery.

Honesty

No legacy is so rich as honesty.
—William Shakespeare

Honesty is vital to our recovery. It has to begin within us and must flow outward from us. To be true to ourselves we must never say one thing and think another. When we were using, our denials spelled dishonesty. So did the false fronts we put up to impress others.

Dishonesty was motivated by fear and our low self-esteem. We hated ourselves, and we were afraid others would hate us, too, if we showed them honestly who we were. So we lied to them and to ourselves, trying to be the person we thought other people wanted us to be. In recovery, we learn to like the person we are. We have no more reason to lie or put up false fronts.

Today I will work to be honest in everything I say and do. I will be true to myself.

Taking Time

Easy does it, but DO it!

—Anonymous

We earnestly believe in "Easy does it." We know that any spiritual progress requires time to grow. Maturity is not an overnight miracle. We need to remember to take things slowly. The faster we rush, the more danger there is of a relapse that could delay vital growth. Only impatient people try to climb ladders several steps at a time.

But we are also taught that slow-but-sure progress does not mean making no effort at all. If we procrastinate, we stop growing and stand still. To delay is to invite rationalization and develop the fear of failing. We seek steady growth by solving problems along the way. We learn from each victory, and take time to enjoy them.

I will remind myself today not to
push myself faster than I need to go.
I won't push the river, I'll let it flow.

Kindness

Have you had a kindness shown? Pass it on.
'Twas not meant for thee alone. Pass it on.
—Henry Burton

Kindness is a priceless possession that returns great dividends when we invest it in our treatment of others. We have corrected our selfishness. We used to care little about others. We showed little kindness. Whenever we show kindness, a share of it stays with us because we are doing something we never dreamed, during our troubled years, was possible. We've learned to be kind to others and ourselves.

Kindness is one of the gifts all of us constantly receive from friends in our program. Kindness knows no permanent home. It passes from one heart to another. There is always room in our lives for more kindness, both to give and to receive.

Today I'll pass on some of the kindness
I've been shown by my friends in the program.

Goals

One who fears, limits their activities. Failure is only the opportunity to more wisely begin again.

—Henry Ford

In sharing with others, especially with our fellow members, we must never be timid about discussing goals, both for a lifetime and for short duration. When we are afraid of failure, we may take no action in setting goals. No one will be scornful of us if we fall short of a mark.

There is more worth in aiming at a target and missing than in shooting blindly. When others encourage us and refuse to let us be depressed by failures, we can take aim and try again. If our goals are realistic, we will reach them. If we fall short, we know we have at least made progress toward our target. The important thing is to aim for the things we need and do our best to get there.

I will set myself realistic goals and work to reach them, but I won't be let down and quit if I fall short. I'll just take better aim next time.

Emotions

All great discoveries are made by men whose feelings run ahead of their thinking.

—C.H. Parkhurst

We spend our time wisely with our fellow members when we talk about our use of emotions. Much pain can be avoided if we learn early not to fear displaying feelings. We can make friends of our emotions, instead of treating them like enemies. Indeed, it is an old saying that emotions taught humanity to reason. We will always need energy to reach goals, and every emotion is a source of energy. None are static.

Power comes from our feelings. Only robots are emotionless. We need *drive* to direct dangerous emotions (like fear and anger) into useful channels and to keep the finer feeling of love and humility from becoming weaknesses by overdoing them. We should always choose positive emotions over negative ones.

I will be most productive in life when I learn that emotional stability is necessary, and that I can FEEL with my mind and THINK with my heart.

Beauty

Though we travel the world over to find the beautiful, we must carry it with us or we find it not.

—Ralph Waldo Emerson

"Beauty" and "beautiful" doesn't just describe the outward appearance of people, places, and things. It also describes inner characteristics. Outer beauty may fade with time, but inner beauty can only grow. It shows in the thoughts, attitudes, and emotions we feel in ourselves and sense in others. It is a necessary part of our spiritual progress.

Beauty becomes a part of our lives when we learn to like who we really care. It is an "outward show of an inner glow."

Beauty also shows itself through goodwill, gratitude, balance, and grace.

I need to remember that building inner beauty through humility, love, gratitude, and services is a necessary part of my spiritual growth.

Change

Change is a process, not an event.
—Anonymous

Recovery from our disease does not happen overnight. We may experience an event that stops our compulsion immediately, but recovery is not an event. There are many more things to do than just stop. We hear some people relate great and dramatic moments of spiritual experience when they are utterly and completely changed. If this is so, we are happy for them. But most of us experience a gradual spiritual awakening.

If we do things in order, we can realize certain benefits. No one element equals change, but all the elements taken together are change. We did not grow up all at once. We will not recover all at once. There is a real joy in our fellowship in watching this process in a newcomer. The slow process of change happens week after week. Sometimes it is like watching the hands of a clock; you don't see them move, but time changes.

My recovery program is based on change as a process and not an event. If change is a single event, then it happens once and it's over. That doesn't allow for continuing growth.

• NOVEMBER 18 •

Came to Believe

Trust God, clean house, help others!
—Anonymous

We have never believed as we are now believing. The process of coming to believe was a restoration to sanity for us. The strength to move into action came from this belief. We needed to accept this Step to start us on the road to recovery. We have made a trip from a dark, lost land to a place of light and beauty.

We were given a new insight and a different kind of knowledge. We came to believe in a Power greater than ourselves, higher than we were, and able to do for us what we couldn't do for ourselves. Once we got that far, a new world of freedom and choice was opened up to us.

When I came to believe in Step Two,
I was introduced to the most transforming
and loving Power I shall ever find. That Power
showed me a way out of my crazy life.

Problems Happen

Today was rough, but that's okay. I used to have years that were rough.

—*Anonymous*

Problems happen whether we are in recovery or not. Recovery does not guarantee us a life free from struggle, pain, or problems. It's not a direct flight to a magically safe place. When we got into our recovery program, the world did not stop and salute us. Recovery is about learning to exist in a world where crummy things can happen.

We are given tools that help us deal with life. The more we use the tools, the better we can live with life's realities and cope. The Twelve Steps, good sponsorship, service work, and especially meetings are tools. Choosing a home group, having a sponsor, and attending meetings give us an ever-present opportunity to handle problems and be with people who can help us. When we have problems and bad days, we no longer need to deal with them by ourselves.

When problems come and upset me, I have learned to get help and talk about them.

Haste

Make haste slowly.
—*Augustus*

It is natural for a newcomer to be impatient and want to know everything possible about recovery quickly. So many efforts have been made in the past toward staying abstinent, with no results, that the addict is sick and tired of the discouragement that followed every failure. As soon as they were aware that success could at long last be theirs, beginners sometimes thought they must waste no time in being experts on the subject of addiction and recovery.

The old saying "haste makes waste" is still good advice. Many a quick learner discovers that when they rush into "educating the whole world" after only a short time in recovery, they often have been looking only at surface truths. Fortunately, such eager beavers quickly learn to dig deeper into the process of admitting and accepting before tackling the job of being a teacher, even to themselves.

When I was new to the program, I needed to remember that I couldn't learn everything overnight. I was told to carry the message, but first I had to find out what it was.

Decision

G.O.D. = Good Orderly Direction
—Anonymous

When we decided to turn our will and lives over to the care of God *as we understood Him*, we made a declaration of independence. We declared our freedom from the chains of our self-centered ego and the unrelenting demands of our self-will. When we decided that God was God and we were not, we began to receive the wonderful future that had been planned for us.

That decision was our claim to a new life. The prison that was our home has been destroyed. We decide to "Let go and let God" on a daily basis. Our wills are always free to decide. We must decide to keep ourselves conscious at all times and listen to the voices that speak to us. We must decide to guard against our ego once again begging to run the show.

My willpower will only be helpful to me when it is acting in accordance with my decision to let my Higher Power instruct me in the way to go.

What If . . .

The lesson I must learn is simply that my control is limited to my own behavior and my own attitudes.

—Anonymous

Many times we try to have knowledge of the will of God before we are ready. Every time we try to guess about tomorrow, we stop living today. All will be revealed to us in due time. The proper hour for an answer will come not a minute too soon nor a minute too late. The only moment we can affect is the present one. When we try to second-guess the future, we feel anxiety.

Thoughts on the future are always done with our worry cap pulled tightly over our ears. We can no longer hear the will of God revealed, because our ears are covered up.

When we play the "what-if" game, we always lose. When we "what if" the future, we create fear and anxiety that runs deep. "What if" will tell us to go backward, to where we are secure and have experience.

I will have faith that God does not play games with me. I won't "what if" tomorrow.

• NOVEMBER 23 •

Fear

The only thing we have to fear is fear itself.
—Franklin D. Roosevelt

Fear was our enemy. It prevented us from living fully. It kept us standing still. It made us close our ears and minds to new ideas and ways of living. Fear of the unknown kept us locked up in our addiction. It told us to stay where it was safe and with what we knew. It refused to let us discover a way to deal with reality.

In recovery, we are learning to cope with fear. We are shown ways to take positive action to get past fear and continue our spiritual progress. Often we find that simply sharing our fears with other members of the program relieves us of them. We have come to realize fear was the spark plug that started our character defects in motion.

I now see how fear kept me a prisoner of my addiction and character defects. I will share my fears with others in the program, and work to get past them. Fear need not always be harmful. It can teach me which direction to go.

Courage

The greatest test of courage on earth is to bear defeat without losing heart.

—Robert Green Ingersoll

One word often heard in group discussions is *will.* Yet the will to do something cannot exist without the action required to do it, and that takes courage. It is courage that turns possibilities into realities and assures us that little in life is truly impossible. Experience teaches us that courage keeps our active emotions under control.

When courage guides our efforts, we can be sure that we will not only be capable of accomplishing success, but we will be worthy of it. We learn that courage is not recklessness; it is common sense. When we know that a goal is worth going for, courage has judgment and carefulness as allies, even though we may be moving against the tide of popular opinion or belief.

I am overcoming my fears about setting and working toward goals. It helps me to remember "courage is fear that has said its prayers."

Complacency

To be nobody but myself—in a world which is doing its best to make us like everyone else—means to fight the hardest battle which any human being can fight and never stop fighting.

—e.e. cummings

Within our fellowship there are many successes that make the member and their loved ones proud. One of the biggest hazards we face is overconfidence, the idea that "I've got it made." This is complacency, an enemy of recovery.

When we're complacent about what we've accomplished, we quit working at progressing. We have to remember that we will never finish our recovery journey. We will always need to keep taking the Steps.

It can be dangerous to let up on the disciplines of the program because things are going well. We need to stay alert and remember that more relapses occur when things are going well than when they're not.

It would be easy to begin feeling like a big shot if I believed all I had to do was achieve one goal, then quit working. I won't give up my fight at staying in recovery.

I'm Sorry

The prayer of amends must be a way of life, not just a sad cry at the end of failure.

—*Anonymous*

Most of us are truly sorry for the wreckage we caused by our behavior. Our disease has touched many people, and the scars sometimes run deep. It would be great if everyone we harmed would accept our apology, but this probably won't happen. It doesn't matter. We still need to tell them we feel bad about their pain.

It's true that we offer amends in the hope of healing relationships. But it is even truer that our recovery depends on our *willingness* to offer amends. Some things can't be set right with an "I'm sorry." We have to show by *actions* as well as *words* that we honestly want to make amends where possible.

As long as I pursue my recovery one day at a time, I will have time enough to demonstrate in action that I am sorry for the pain I caused.

Rebels

Some people never grow up—
they just grow old.
—Anonymous

As a group, most of us were rebellious and defiant. We lived for excitement, kicks, and highs. We liked living on the edge. We were outlaws from society. The fast lane wasn't fast enough. We weren't satisfied with getting high or too high; we wanted to be *way* too high. "Live fast, die young" was our motto.

For many of us, "acting out" got us in trouble with authority. We didn't like authority figures or anyone who tried to influence our behavior. In recovery, we have learned that our rebellious attitude and behavior was just a sign of immaturity. We became aware that our defiance and grandiosity had no place in recovery. Now we cooperate with life. We aren't banging our heads against walls anymore.

I have come to see my rebellion as having no place in my recovery. I don't want to be an outlaw anymore.

Saying No

The art of being wise is the art of knowing what to overlook.

— William James

One of our common goals in recovery is balance, a feeling of being centered. If we lean too far in one direction, we lose our balance and fall over. We can't please everyone. We can't be everything to everybody. There is a balance, the program teaches us, between selfishness and selflessness.

We need to be careful to organize our time and set priorities. We can't sponsor everyone, be at every meeting, or volunteer for every service opportunity. Recovery is not a race to see who can do the most. "Easy does it." We need to learn and practice what are called "refusal skills." We need to learn when to say no. We have the right to refuse requests, to slow down and take time out, to take care of ourselves.

I let myself get too stressed out when I'm not careful in scheduling my time.

Bridges

People are lonely because they build walls instead of bridges.
—Joseph Newton

We discovered—and hardly believed it at first—that we were not alone. We were really not that different from everybody else in the program. We began to sense that we did belong somewhere, and our loneliness began to leave us. Our addiction encouraged us to build walls around ourselves, to keep out reality and to keep in the awful person we thought we were. When we began recovery, we started to tear down those walls, brick by brick. On the foundation that was left, we have started to build a new life.

That new life is connected to the real world, to other people, and to the program by the bridges we've built with our positive actions. We've learned that with honesty and sharing, we no longer need walls to protect us.

I am learning to tear down the walls I have built and have begun to build bridges.

Meditation

If thou may not continually gather thyself together, do it some time at least once a day.

— *Thomas à Kempis*

For all of us who take meditation seriously, the real purpose is to improve our conscious contact with our Higher Power. But when we meditate, we are also giving ourselves time to digest the rich rewards we find in the program. We begin our day with a quiet time of prayer, meditation, and reflection. We take the time at night to review our day, to see the things we might improve, to remember the things we did well and enjoy them.

Meditation is a quiet time in a noisy world. It is a chance to talk with our Higher Power and to listen for answers to our questions. It's an opportunity in the evening to let stress and tension flow away, and to regain serenity. Meditation is a time of healing.

Today I will also remember that meditation heals me from the scars of a busy, noisy world, and lets me return to serenity, just as it helps me with my conscious contact with my Higher Power.

DECEMBER

Sanity

Insanity is repeating the same mistake and expecting different results.

—Anonymous

Our old world of an out-of-control self-will was strange and crazy. Everything was turned around: right was left, up was down, good was bad, white was black, night was day. We could trust in nothing, because nothing trusted us. We believed in nothing, because nothing believed in us. We loved nothing, because nothing loved us. We became cruel and mean-spirited. We lived life always on the defensive.

The more we acted on the strength of our own ego, the smaller our world became. Finally, in desperation, we shut everyone and everything out. Then we were truly isolated, living in a make-believe world filled with dragons, monsters, and ghosts. Our ego had painted us into a corner, and our lives had become unmanageable.

I learned the way to stop my craziness in my Second Step. My sanity has been restored.

Prayer

Prayer is the voice of faith.
—William Van Horne

Prayer is what we do before we act, not after. Prayer is our choice of whose team we are on. Since we no longer take on the job of coach, we listen when we pray. We want to hear the call of each new play. We want to hear our assignment. When it comes time to act, we act according to the plan for us. This kind of prayer helps to bring us results.

When we ask only to do God's will, we cannot fail. Sometimes when we pray, we discover great things are being asked of us. We wonder where we will get the strength and the determination to succeed. Remember, we are never asked for more than we can do. Our Higher Power understands our potential better than we do. Sometimes when we pray we discover our role is different from the one we thought it was.

I have not been the best judge of what is good for me. I trust the answers to my prayers because my Higher Power wants only what is best for me.

Fellowship

Our program is not something you join; it is a way of life.
—Anonymous

There is a rich, deep fellowship in our program. We have discovered friendships beyond anything we ever experienced before. The meetings we attend, the people we sponsor, the coffee we pour, the service we perform—all make up the experience. But the fellowship is not an organization; the fellowship is the coming together of a group of men and women who share a way of life. This way of life is based on certain Steps and Traditions.

We participate in the fellowship to better work our Steps and live the Traditions. We recover as we live this new way of life. We add to the fellowship when we bring this life to the meetings. We cannot expect anyone to live our lives for us. If we do not do our work, we will have nothing to share.

In sharing, I give back what I have so freely taken. The fellowship teaches me that my recovery is found in the Steps and Traditions. When I put them all together, I have a new way of life.

Yeah, But . . .

Nothing is easy to the unwilling.
— Thomas Fuller

Just as a person does not "sort of" get pregnant, or "sort of" get married, we don't "sort of" do the will of our Higher Power. The program is one of honesty. Where there were once half-steps, now there are full Steps. We had allowed our disease to dictate the terms of all our relationships. This meant everything had to come second to our addiction. Every action was conditioned on our ability to feed our problem.

Now that we are in recovery, we are asked, "Are we willing to go to *any* lengths?" If we do not answer with a loud yes, we set ourselves up for failure. There is no "yeah, but . . ." when we follow the Steps and the instructions of our sponsor. There is no reading between the lines when we practice the principles of our program.

"Yeah, but . . ." responses are dangerous for me because they mean I'm not listening or moving forward. When I hear myself say it, I should ask for help in removing the "but."

Believing

When we surrendered to our Higher Power, the journey began.

—*Anonymous*

Many of us had trouble believing that a God existed when we began our recovery program, because for years we thought we were the master of our own affairs. We paid attention to no desires or wishes but our own.

When we realized how much help we needed, we first looked to other members and our group for support. By rejecting at first the idea of a Power *higher* than ourselves, many of us did accept the idea of a Power *other* than ourselves. As we have made spiritual progress, most of us now have a clear and ongoing belief in a Higher Power that we call God.

It is important to our recovery to rely on God, as our own belief in a Higher Power is what can and does save us from our addiction. Only two of the Steps talk about addiction. The other ten talk about spiritual growth.

I have a firm foundation for spiritual health and spiritual progress when I continue to believe in my Higher Power.

Spiritual

Spirituality is at the heart of the Twelve Step program of recovery. There is not a spiritual part of the program. It is a spiritual program.
—*Jerry Dollard*

A person who has had a spiritual experience does not wear that experience on their sleeve. What the fellowship has discovered about the spirit has nothing to do with a "holier than thou" attitude. A spiritual person is surrounded by peace and tranquility. They are busy with life, living each moment fully. They have an active concern with the well-being of other people.

A spiritual person may be surrounded by turmoil and still have serenity. The spiritual experience causes us to act differently. We are less concerned about ourselves. We know that we are well provided for. We are told to remember, "When we got to the place where there was nothing left but God, we found that God was enough."

My spiritual growth has helped me, through my attitudes and actions, to better live with myself, my Higher Power, and others.

Humility

We come nearest to the great when we are great in humility.

—Rabindranath Tagore

No single characteristic brings us greater joy than humility. There is no greater defense against the cunning, baffling, and powerful disease with which we live. We must learn to understand the strength and wisdom that come from a truly humble person.

It is good to get rid of our misconceptions about humility. Humility has nothing to do with shyness, weakness, or putting ourselves down. When humility becomes an ego-booster, then it turns into a character defect. Humility is living in a proper relationship to God. When we walk with God, we don't have to try to be humble. We *are* humble.

The reason there is strength and power in humility is that God is strong and powerful. My own daily abstinence is but one result of this Power.

Surrender

In my end is my beginning.
—T.S. Eliot

Don't just quit, surrender! We now know there is a big difference. Most of us quit a thousand times. We bet all we had on our ability to just say no. Each morning, with a swollen head, we made our pledge to quit. Then as the sun began to go down, the memory of the quitting faded away, and we were again deep into our addiction. The rock-solid purpose we had in the morning had utterly dissolved in the evening.

We couldn't quit because we were out of control and living in denial. Our only hope was in surrendering to our powerlessness and admitting that we could not *will* this monkey away. What came before surrender was the acknowledgment that there was someone to whom we were surrendering. We did not need to worry about naming the force or the Power that was in control.

I needed only to surrender and let go of
the will that tormented me on a daily basis.
The answer came in my act of surrender.

Transformation

Progress is a nice word. But change is its motivator.

—Robert F. Kennedy

We humbly ask God in our Seventh Step to remove our shortcomings. We are asking God to do in other parts of our lives what He has done to our addiction. Each moment we experience freedom from our disease, we acknowledge God's power. Many of us lost our desire for our addiction quickly. Others waged a long and painful battle to reach a point of surrender. How will God work on our shortcomings? Will it be immediate, or will it be over time?

Our fellowship suggests that we live our lives one day at a time. Personal change occurs but one day at a time. We must resist the temptation to set God's clock to fast forward. The long-sought-after changes will occur in ways we cannot predict and should not expect.

I have not been the best judge as to what is good for me. I must trust God in all things, even those that are most personal to me.

Glamorizing

I'm slipping when I begin to remember
more of the good times than the bad.

—Anonymous

We must keep our memories of the years before the program in proper perspective. By the grace of God the compulsion was released from us. However, the addiction was not removed; it is always waiting for us to lower our guard. A danger sign we watch for is the voice that rewrites our past history.

The scenes we remember are parties, new partners, romance, laughter, music, sex, ballgames, intimate conversations, poolside play, Sunday brunch, getting ready to go out and party hearty. Seldom do we remember the bleary-eyed mornings, the waking up with horrible strangers, the embarrassments, the lost jobs, wrecked cars, wet beds, the toilet-hugging, the divorce that broke our hearts.

When my addiction talks to me about
the good times, I need to remember
the rest of the story.

Forgiveness

I'm slipping when I say forgive,
but don't forget.

—*Anonymous*

When we join in an act of forgiveness, we bring relationships whole again. Forgiveness is not a state of mind. It is a state of being. If we do not forgive deep within our hearts, we have not really forgiven. Forgiveness that stays up in the head is really only the intention to forgive.

We know we have not truly forgiven when we can't forget what caused our resentments. If this wound is still open and sore, we did not forgive from the heart. We remember to give ourselves time, talk with our sponsor and fellow members, and pray for help. It is good to share our resentment in a meeting and ask for suggestions. Finally we must wait. God will heal the wound in time *if we let Him.*

My willingness is the key. If I am
willing to let go, I will be given
the power to truly forgive.

• DECEMBER 12 •

Defects

The greatest of all faults, I should say,
is to be conscious of none.
—Thomas Carlyle

One of the first things we heard in our program was that we probably had defects of character. We first admitted we were powerless over a substance or behavior. Then we learned that those who believed they had no faults of character were mistaken. Little progress could be made without looking at our defects of character.

Such a self-analysis, in order to be thorough, must include assets. But the big challenge is to understand our faults and to use the other Steps of the program to get rid of them. We are not, never were, and never will be candidates for sainthood. We never try to be perfect but give continual attention to character growth.

By doing my inventory on a daily basis,
I make myself aware of my character defects
and what I need to do to grow out of them.

Envy

There is not a passion so strongly rooted in the human heart as envy.

—Richard Sheridan

In the past when we drank, used, or misbehaved, our self-worth was beaten down to the point of feeling less than everyone around us. We wallowed in feelings of worthlessness, awkwardness, sadness, and self-pity. We were envious of those who had what we wanted.

Envy brought hatred, jealousy, anger, fear, disrespect, and distrust. We wished failure and disaster on people who had become successful or had gained in any way.

Before the program, we wanted what others had, but we didn't know how to get it. Now we're happy with the miracles we receive in recovery. We have discovered that doing is more important than having and experiencing is more important than possessing.

Today I'll remember when I practice love, caring, and sharing, I experience little envy.

Spade Work

Count your garden by the flowers,
not by the leaves that fall.

—Dixie Willson

Stories we hear as lessons should be shared with friends so they, too, can benefit from them. One such tale is about a young woman seeking spiritual growth.

When told, "You weren't promised a rose garden," she replied, "No, but I appreciate the garden I've been given. I know I'll never enjoy lovely roses unless I personally spend much time weeding, hoeing, mulching, fertilizing, watering, spraying, and pruning. Only after working in my garden can I pause to smell the roses. And if I am unwilling to risk getting stuck by thorns, I'll never have the joy of gathering beautiful flowers to give to those I love."

Life is like a garden. Enjoyment of it
depends on how well I do the spade work.
Many an old-timer reminds me "pray for
potatoes, but pick up a hoe."

Servants

A servant who made service seem divine.
—Henry Wadsworth Longfellow

The recognition of the fact that we have servants to make growth possible is one of the first great discoveries that developed when we joined a Twelve Step group. These servants are as genuine as the sense of love that makes us truly sharing and caring people. Without the emotional servants that make possible changes in attitudes, we could never reach a new style in living. These servants are positive and active.

If the first thing we hear when we reach for recovery is "let us love you until you can learn to love yourself," the second may well be, "honesty begins within your own self." We recognize a long list of helping hands that join in steering us toward a comfortable recovery. These hands join in helping us find the way toward that wonderful destination.

My servants are the tools I find when I enter my program. Some of them are called gratitude, perseverance, vigilance, belief, humility, tolerance, and acceptance. I must count the many, many more.

Don't Judge

Don't judge anyone until you have walked a mile in their shoes.

—*Anonymous*

God did not make different classes of human beings. It has taken people several thousand years to understand this fact. Even now, the understanding is not always practiced. We learn in our recovery that we are all equal in our ability to be human.

Recovery from our disease does not free us from being human. It gives us a way of life to deal *with* this fact. For there to be serenity and peace in our lives, we have to learn to accept our humanness.

If people act as we think they shouldn't, then we have to change the way we think. It is just that simple. The acceptance we seek goes beyond things and events. The Serenity Prayer also refers to people as well as things. We are really asking our Higher Power to accept people as they *are*. We can't change them.

Today I'll remember to live and let live. This removes me from the position of judging others.

Meetings

It takes the good and bad meeting—the good and bad speaker—to make the program work.

—*Anonymous*

We are told that every meeting we attend will be a good meeting. Our sponsor will tell us that there are no bad meetings; all meetings are good, some are just better than others. Newcomers are asked not to even consider whether the meetings are good or bad. "Just bring your body and the mind will follow," and "take what you need and leave the rest."

Even when we think we didn't get much out of a meeting, we will find that many others who were there benefited a great deal. We may remember something we heard at a "bad" meeting more often than what we heard at a "good" meeting. The old-timers tell us, "The most important part of any meeting, for you, is the moment you walk through the door into it. It's not so much what you do there, it's the fact that you are there."

Today I'll remember some meetings may be better than others, but it's more important that I'm there.

Past Mistakes

If you turn it over and don't let go of it, you'll be upside down.

—Anonymous

A lot of unhappiness comes from dwelling on past mistakes and failures. Our Higher Power can do many things for us: remove a lifelong compulsion to drink, to drug, to overeat, to gamble; and remove all kinds of character defects such as lying, cheating, stealing, adultery. God can determine many things, but our Higher Power cannot force us to accept our past. If we choose to walk around with shame and guilt about the past, that's our choice.

It has been the collective wisdom of our fellowship that many people have relapsed because they couldn't let go and accept their past mistakes. We all, each one of us, were born imperfect. It is not surprising that this imperfection, along with our addiction, has caused us trouble along the way.

I learn how to live with my past mistakes by practicing and using the tools of my program.

The Steps

There are Twelve Steps in the
ladder to continued recovery.
—Anonymous

Is there such a thing as partial recovery? Can a person work just a few Steps and leave the rest? Can we just "sort of" do a Fourth Step, like in our minds? Do we really have to write it down as we are instructed? Can we do our Fifth Step with our dog or cat or a favorite tree?

Can we make an amend just in our minds? Can we ask someone to make an amend for us? A person we can't stand has asked us to be their sponsor. Can we say no? We feel much better about our lives now that we are in recovery, but we really can't do some of these Steps because they're too hard.

I have heard such questions and listened to such declarations. I know the facts are quite simple. Those that didn't work all the Steps DIDN'T make it. Those that do work all the Steps DO make it.

Recovery Mask

It's easy to fool other people. Fooling yourself is a little harder. Fooling God is impossible.

—Chris Harrison

The question often arises in the program as to why "so and so" relapsed after time in recovery. The answer is *dishonesty*. Most of us agree that before we came into the program, we hid behind a mask and didn't let anyone really know us. Since coming into the program, some of us hide behind the dreaded "Recovery Mask."

When someone is wearing a Recovery Mask, they deceive others into believing that they're doing well in recovery. The real danger lies in deceiving themselves into believing the same thing. One thing this false image can't live with is truth. It would be helpful for them to ask themselves, "When was the last time I shared what was really going on inside me, in my innermost world, with somebody, my sponsor, or my home group?"

It does me harm to hide behind a Recovery Mask. If I do, I may relapse because I'm not sharing my experience, strength, and hope, but only my opinions, attitudes, and advice.

Service

In about the same degree as you are helpful, you will be happy.

— Karl Reiland

The service work we are called to do in Step Twelve is a result of our spiritual awakening. When most of us thought of service, we thought of restaurant help, chores around the house, washing windows. The thought of service was burdensome if not downright irritating. We probably schemed throughout our lives to do as little service as possible. Every moment we gave to someone else was one less moment we could spend on ourselves. This stands to reason, for we were totally self-centered. Even those of us who "acted as if" we cared normally received much more than we ever gave.

The Twelve Step way of life produces selflessness. We, by the grace of God, care less about ourselves and more about our fellows.

When I pass on my recovery, I keep it. This spiritual paradox becomes an all-determining reality for me, that to keep what I have found, I must give it away. Service becomes a way of life.

Consistency

We cannot remain consistent with the world save by growing inconsistent with our past selves.

—Havelock Ellis

Mathematics is a science of formulas. These formulas always give us consistent results. Two plus two is consistently four. The universe is a place of consistency.

There is something to be said for consistency in our own lives. It is wonderful when we do not have to wake up each morning and invent new identities like a fugitive, or invent a new game plan like a con man.

It is a great feeling when we are not fighting the universe each day. When we know our role and choose to play that role with all our energies, we are each of great and lasting value.

It is very important that I do the job I have been assigned. My universe depends on my actions to work properly. My consistent behavior makes my whole universe run smoothly.

Prompt Admission

Timeliness is best in all matters.
—Hesiod

If we happened to be a certain NASA scientist, we know all about prompt admissions. In the late 1970s, when the Voyager spacecraft was sent into space to explore the planets of our solar system, something happened shortly after liftoff. One of the scientists noticed the path of the rocket was off by one ten-thousandth of a degree. It was a very small mistake, but unless the mistake was corrected early, it would multiply itself many times over.

Instead of hitting a target one billion miles away, the craft would miss the mark and the mission would fail. The mistake was corrected, and success was assured.

So it is with our daily inventory. We take prompt and immediate action so we can stay on target. Our target is our conscious contact with God.

When I stray off course, even slightly, I take prompt action to right myself. What appears at the moment to be a minor wrong can quickly grow and jeopardize my recovery.

Holidays

Keep your recovery First to make it Last.
—Anonymous

We all encounter places, people, and times of the year that trigger memories of our old lifestyle, pleasant or painful events. Holidays and family gatherings may be especially stressful times for us.

There have always been a lot of expectations associated with holidays. Many of us may feel pressured to fulfill those expectations. We need to remember that it is a naturally stressful time, and we may feel more nervous than usual. We can avoid forcing moods or events on ourselves or those around us.

In recovery, we are given tips that have helped many members during the holidays. We plan extra program activities and keep our phone list handy. We skip any slippery occasions that make us uneasy. We attend special program events. We take a fellow member with us to a possibly slippery party if we feel uncomfortable going alone.

When I keep my recovery Number One in my mind, the holidays, with the help of my friends, will be enjoyable and less stressful.

Promises

A promise made is a debt unpaid.
—Robert W. Service

We often hear about and read the promises. As we finish reading the list of rewards, we come upon a sentence that asserts that all these promises will materialize if we, who are looking for spiritual growth, work for the rewards. We can direct our efforts carefully by knowing *what* is happening and by being among those who are *making* things happen.

Thus we discover that none of the promises bring us outright gifts. They must actually not even be anticipated or expected. We who are looking for promised things are actually our own solution. The rewards are accepted with humility and gratefulness. We must always believe that we have earned the promised results.

The natural growth I experience in all the events of life arrive with a focus on spiritual growth. Gifts come in their natural time and cannot be rushed or postponed, but I must always work for them.

Ability

We came to the program to stop our addiction.
What we found was a way to start living.

—*Anonymous*

We all have within ourselves the ability to maintain recovery. To begin with, all that was needed was a desire to stop. Most of us, before admitting our powerlessness, were possessed by the fear that we were helpless and hopeless. We had tried to quit many times and always failed.

For years, addictions were considered the stamp of doom. It was true that addicts were incurable, but wise men and women kept crying out that obsessions could be arrested. The ability to keep winning is within all of us who have faith and belief that we can. Recovery is a constant challenge for us all. Those who accept the challenge have discovered that the program is simple but not always easy. Ability always follows surrender to reality.

With the strength provided by the fellowship,
my sponsor, and my Higher Power, I know
I have the ability to maintain recovery.

Relationships

Love doesn't just sit there, like a stone;
it has to be made, like bread, remade
all the time, made new.

— *Ursula K. LeGuin*

We all probably believe our recovery program will give us new chances to form relationships. This may be frightening to us because our experience with intimate friendships has been pretty rocky. They have been a source of much pain and misery for many of us. We have only to look around to see that, for most people, relationships are not easy.

When we work our Steps, we discover how much shame, guilt, pity, and anger we had for ourselves and our partners. We had invested enormous amounts of time, energy, and personal resources in those relationships. The program has revealed a need to completely overhaul our attitudes about intimate and personal relations.

The program has helped me be a better partner in a relationship. Most of the time I never really needed better partners. I just needed to be a better person.

Moving Away

I'm slipping when I begin to dislike the company and conversation of the program.

—*Anonymous*

There is a reason why a lamb gets separated from a flock. The flock will be eating on a particular pasture, and a lamb will take a fancy to grass just off to the edge of the field. So the lamb takes a little nibble of this grass. Then he moves just ever so slightly farther from the edge and takes another little nibble, then just a bit farther and another nibble.

Each little nibble of grass takes the lamb farther and farther from the flock. After a while, having eaten enough grass, the lamb pokes his head up and notices that the flock has left him. "B-A-A-A-A-A!" the lamb wails. How could his flock have left him?

I will begin slipping when I stop paying attention to my flock. My group will not leave me; if I leave my group, it will be like the lamb, just one conversation, one meeting at a time. After a while I, too, could end up wailing for help just like the little lamb.

Meetings

I'm slipping when I'm willing to stay away from meetings.

—Anonymous

Being in too big a hurry to get well can present problems for us. When we are in a hurry, our eyes focus on the destination, not the journey. We are anxious to get somewhere, rather than become something. The fellowship is more like a sailboat than a power boat. The power that propels us is one we have no control over. The controls are somewhere else, and the pilot is somebody else.

Meetings are not the means to an end. Meetings are an end themselves, a way of life. Each meeting is its own reward. We hear people talk of a meeting being one stone in the foundation of our recovery. If we have accumulated many of these stones, when temptation comes our way, we will have built a good foundation to say no.

Since I am never cured, I remember that "When I want to go to a meeting, I can walk, and when I don't I should run."

No Easy Solution

There is no chemical solution
to a spiritual problem.

—Anonymous

We are faced with a dilemma in recovery. On the one hand, we have a physical disease that will kill us if it is not treated. On the other hand, medical science knows of no cure for our physical malady. The real problem for us is spiritual in nature. That is why the medical profession can't cure us. Until we treat the symptoms, there can be no cure. The solution to the real problem is the long-term treatment of our spiritual lives, and this can only begin when we quit using.

We have watched men and women stop without getting into recovery. Their lives do not become that much better. They are usually said to be on a "dry drunk." The stoppage of the disease halts its progression. The recovery program promotes long-term treatment.

What an order! I can't go through with this. There is no easier, softer way. There is no pill I can take to make me better. There is no substance-induced solution to a spiritual problem.

The Program

And practice these principles in all our affairs.
—*Big Book of Alcoholics Anonymous*

The longer we are on the program, the more we enrich all parts of our lives. There is hardly a topic mentioned that does not allow us to learn. It is not that we become progressively dumber in recovery; it is just that we become progressively more open-minded. We seem to be hungry for growth opportunities.

We are not timid about meeting new people and taking part in new recovery experiences. When we have an opportunity to share our experience, strength, and hope, we do so with gratitude and humility. We can't be arrogant about our progress. We know that false pride is dangerous for us. Others have taken too much credit for recovery and lost it.

When I practice these principles, I acknowledge my powerlessness; believe and trust in my Higher Power; keep a clear, clean conscience; talk with my sponsor; maintain a willingness to change; have a humble attitude; maintain a daily inventory; pray and meditate; attend meetings; and pass it on.

Sanskrit Proverb

Look to this day,
For it is life,
The very life of life.
In its brief course lies all
The realities and verities of existence,
The bliss of growth,
The splendor of action,
The glory of power—

For yesterday is but a dream
And tomorrow is only a vision.
But today, well lived,
Makes every yesterday
a dream of happiness
And every tomorrow
a vision of hope.

Look well, therefore, to this day.

Prayer of St. Francis of Assisi

Lord, make me an instrument
of Your peace!
Where there is hatred, let me sow love.
Where there is injury, pardon.
Where there is doubt, faith.
Where there is despair, hope.
Where there is darkness, light.
Where there is sadness, joy.

O Divine Master,
grant that I may not so much seek
To be consoled as to console.
To be understood as to understand.
To be loved as to love.
For it is in giving
that we receive.
It is in pardoning
that we are pardoned.
It is in dying
that we are born to eternal life.

Inventory Checklist

LIABILITIES *Watch for*	**ASSETS** *Strive for*
Anger	Calmness
Anxiety/worry	Serenity
Argumentativeness	Cooperation
Boredom	Action
Closed-mindedness	Open-mindedness
Complacency	Action
Confusion	Clarity
Controlling	Surrender
Criticizing	Look for the good
Denial	Acceptance
Dishonesty	Honesty
Doubt	Belief
Egotism	Humility
Envy	Kindness
False pride	Healthy pride
Fantasizing	Reality
Fear	Faith
Grandiosity	Self-confidence
Hate	Love
Immaturity	Maturity
Impatience	Patience
Impulsiveness	Self-control
Insincerity	Sincerity
Intolerance	Tolerance
Irresponsibility	Responsibility

Eliminate the Negative	Accentuate the Positive
Isolation	Helping others
Jealousy	Trust
Laziness	Activity
Low self-esteem	Self-worth
Negative attitude	Positive attitude
Perfectionism	Being human
Phoniness	Being yourself
Procrastination	Promptness
Projecting	Here and now
Resentment	Forgiveness
Rigidity	Flexibility
Sadness	Happiness
Self-centeredness	Other-centeredness
Self-doubt	Self-acceptance
Self-importance	Modesty
Self-indulgence	Discipline
Selfishness	Sharing
Self-pity	Self-forgetfulness
Shame	Self-respect
Stinking thinking	Healthy thinking
Stubbornness	Willingness
Vulgar/immoral	Spiritual

Subject Index

E

F

G

H

M

N

O

P

Q

R

S

T

U

V

W

Y

About Hazelden Publishing

As part of the Hazelden Betty Ford Foundation, Hazelden Publishing offers both cutting-edge educational resources and inspirational books. Our print and digital works help guide individuals in treatment and recovery, and their loved ones. Professionals who work to prevent and treat addiction also turn to Hazelden Publishing for evidence-based curricula, digital content solutions, and videos for use in schools, treatment programs, correctional programs, and electronic health records systems. We also offer training for implementation of our curricula.

Through published and digital works, Hazelden Publishing extends the reach of healing and hope to individuals, families, and communities affected by addiction and related issues.

Other Titles That May Interest You

Cornerstones

Daily Meditations for the Journey into Manhood and Recovery

VICTOR LA CERVA, MD

This collection of daily readings—specifically designed for men new to recovery or working to move beyond internal roadblocks that prevent true personal evolution—offers guidance, inspiration, spirituality, affirmation, and new definitions of manhood for building a life free from substance use and addictions.

Order No. 3518 (softcover); also available as an ebook

Stepping Stones

More Daily Meditations for Men

FROM THE BEST-SELLING AUTHOR OF *TOUCHSTONES*

In the spiritual successor to the best-selling *Touchstones*, the author continues to explore masculinity and sobriety. *Stepping Stones* offers insight into the many roles men undertake—father and son, friend and lover—and provides actionable meditations for leading a full life despite its chaos.

Order No. 5859 (softcover); also available as an e-book

Keep It Simple
Daily Meditations for Twelve Step Beginnings and Renewal

Life can be complicated and hectic, but when we keep things simple, we can bring them down to a manageable size. These meditations—loved by millions over their three decades in print—focus on the Twelve Steps, stressing the importance of putting into practice new beliefs, slogans, and fellowship.

Order No. 5066; also available as an e-book